MEDITATIONS ON THE LETTERS OF PAUL

EXERCISES IN BIBLICAL THEOLOGY

HEROLD WEISS

Energion Publications
Gonzalez, FL
2016

Copyright © 2016, Herold Weiss

Unless otherwise noted, scripture quotations are from the Revised Standard Version of the Bible, copyright 1952 [2nd edition, 1971] by the Division of Christian Education of the National Council of the Churches of Christ in the United States of America. Used by permission. All rights reserved.

Cover Design: Henry E. Neufeld

ISBN10: 1-63199-222-8
ISBN13: 978-1-63199-222-3
Library of Congress Control Number: 2016935327

Energion Publications
P. O. Box 841
Gonzalez, FL 32560
Energion.com

About *Meditations on the Letters of Paul*

Dr. Weiss's book truly captures the spirit of the Apostle Paul. Paul comes alive in this text, which addresses the whole person and not just the intellect. Dr. Weiss invites the reader to experience Paul's vision and understand the historical settings that inspired Paul's Letters. Readers will discover a living Paul, imperfect yet insightful, mystical yet practical, activist yet contemplative, and evangelical yet universalist. This text is a creative addition to the literature on Paul. It is scholarly, yet accessible to the committed layperson. It deserves to stand in the company of Pauline texts such as those penned N.T. Wright, Marcus Borg, John Dominic Crossan, and Jouette Bassler. This text will inspire pastors, professors, seminarians, and educated laypersons.

    – **Bruce Epperly, PhD**, author of *Experiencing God in Suffering: A Journey with Job, Philippians: A Participatory Study Guide*, and *Process Theology: Embracing Adventure with God*

Weiss has done more than summing up Paul's theology under seventeen chapters, each titled after a fundamental Christian doctrine largely formulated by the Apostle. Having crystallized the complex network of thoughts in the Letters, and displaying thorough familiarity with the literature devoted to them, he draws his readers into these well-considered beliefs—in historical context and for our times. A must-read book even for those who have explained Paul's understanding of Christ and the implications of the cross.

    – **Abraham Terian, PhD**, St. Nersess Armenian Seminary

Dr. Weiss well named this book *Meditations*, for it is to be savored in small servings, not digested all at once. Have your Bible at hand, for you will be driven to reread it with new and refreshing insights. He lets Paul speak for himself. The chapters/themes build on one another so that each turns back upon itself to create a fullness that brings Paul fully to life. What ensues is a cohesive summary of his major themes, chapter by chapter. Weiss moves effortlessly from Paul's apocalyptic worldview to our day making Paul relevant then and now.

Weiss does not restate tired observations, but recreates Paul as a man, a Jew of his time. In doing so, we are offered a side of Paul not often seen, one quite different from the traditional Pauline theology of the Reformation. He gives us a real man whose struggles to understand the Christ event pitted him against his own people, his churches, and even himself. The result broadens not only our understanding of the apostle, but of ourselves, and the meaning of our faith.

– **Rev. Steve Kindle,** Director, Clergy United
Author of *I'm Right and You're Wrong:
Why We Disagree about the Bible and What to Do about It*

Paul the theologian was also Paul the pastor. He brought his deep theological convictions about Jesus and the gospel to bear on the pastoral concerns of his audience. Harold Weiss understands that and help us to understand it in this book.

I invite you to read the reflections in these pages to gain a new and/or renewed perspective on the great Apostle, who has been the most influential theologian/pastor of the Christian faith throughout the centuries.

– **Allan R. Bevere,** Pastor
Team Ministry and Professional Fellow in Theology, Ashland Theological Seminary, Ashland, Ohio

Herold Weiss's meditations on Pauline thought are ideal introductions to this influetial, but complex and often misunderstood early Christian figure. Weiss is a steady, careful, and insightful guide who provides the pefect amount of background and attention to interpretive issues to help tease out Paul's theology buried in his authentic letters. And as a bonus, the book is a pleasure to read.

– **Ruben Dupertuis, PhD**
Trinity University

Dedicated to the memory
of
Roland E. Loasby
1890 – 1974
an inimitable and most effective teacher
of the exegesis of Greek texts.
He taught me how, with unforgettable precision and humor,
to read the New Testament texts
and get it.

Table of Contents

	Preface	vii
	Introduction	1
I	My Gospel	13
II	Faith, Hope and Love	25
III	The Holy Spirit that has been Given to Us	35
IV	We are Children of Promise	41
V	Keep Your Hearts and Your Minds	49
VI	God Sent Forth His Son	63
VII	God is Faithful	75
VIII	By Which Law?	89
IX	All Have Sinned	99
X	The Obedience of Faith	111
XI	The Life I Now Live in the Flesh	119
XII	Glorify God in your Body	129
XIII	I have made Myself a Slave to All	141
XIV	The Creation Itself Will Be Set Free	147
XV	I Press On Toward the Goal	159
XVI	The Day of Christ	173
XVII	When I Am Weak, Then I Am Strong	185
	Epilogue	197
	Index of References to the Letters of Paul	209

Preface

My first book, *Paul of Tarsus: His Gospel and Life*, was published in 1986. The first printing was soon exhausted. That gave me the opportunity to publish an expanded revised edition in 1989. That second edition has been sold out for a number of years. A few years back a friend suggested to me that I should write a new revised edition and offered his help for the project. After giving the matter some consideration I decided not to pursue it. At the time I had other projects that needed my attention.

When I finished writing *Meditations on* According to John: *Exercises in Biblical Theology*, I thought I should write a companion volume on the letters of Paul. As I mention in the Preface to *According to John*, I had wanted to write a book on that gospel for a long time, but I could not come up with the appropriate structure for the book. Once I came up with the format and actually wrote the book, I felt that I had also found the way to give my reading of the letters of Paul a satisfactory new dress. A lot of water has run under the bridge since 1989; therefore, I could no longer use the schema I had used back then. While on some things my mind has remained the same, in some important ways, as I considered the evidence after many years of theological reflection, I have changed my mind.

Around 1999, my colleague at Northern Seminary, Charles Cosgrove, invited me to write with him and K. K. Yeo, a professor at Northwestern University, a book that would look at Paul's letters from different cultural locations. Since each of us had grown up in a different culture, each wrote a chapter reading Paul in terms of his own culture, and then another chapter from a culture other than his own. The idea was to exhibit the influence of cultures and the difficulties and the rewards of trying to see things in terms of other cultures. The book, *Cross-Cultural Paul: Journeys to Others, Journeys to Ourselves,* offers six different cultural readings of Paul and draws some conclusions from the exercise. Writing my chapters of that book certainly taught me to pay more attention to Paul's own culture. That was something I had not paid much attention to in my first book.

My meditations on Paul's letters are attempts to come to terms with how Paul's mind works, what are his basic presuppositions, what is peculiarly his when handling issues also considered by others. In this effort I have not been primarily concerned with treating everything he wrote, but to see how what he wrote holds together around central ideas. In my meditations, I have tried to understand Paul in his own terms as well as I possibly can. Hopefully, my struggles with Paul will also bear fruit for others. Trying to understand his struggles with his contemporaries is the best way to gain insights into his fruitful, creative mind. Again, I call these exercises "meditations" because rather than trying to use Paul to construct my version of the Gospel I am trying to come to terms with his Gospel, and that requires to chew slowly and carefully what he wrote in order to get to its core.

As I have pointed out elsewhere, writing is not quite a lonely affair, even if it requires a fair amount of personal concentration. As a writer, I always have with me my audience, even if only in my imagination. Traditionally, "meditations," be they those of Marcus Aurelius or of Descartes, are attempts to express fundamental things not just for oneself, but with others in mind. The audience is what gives their writing a distinctive tone. Friends of mine have read these meditations as they were written and offered criticism, comments, suggestions and encouragement. At times they have suggested how to say something better, at others they have pointed out the implications or the consequences of my interpretation. I owe a great deal to my Saint Mary's colleague, Terence Martin. He has been a long-standing friend and effective sound board through the years. His generous observations and suggestions have been most helpful in the writing of this book. Jean and Don Rhoads have again been most selfless with their time and effort to make sure that my writing was clear and in good English. Finally I must thank Henry Neufeld, my publisher, for his encouragement and support. This is the fourth book of mine he is publishing. I am most grateful for his enthusiasm for the project and the professionalism with which he has carried it forward.

The book is dedicated to Roland Loasby, the professor of Greek exegesis of the New Testament who opened my eyes to the advantage and the value of reading what the biblical authors wrote in the original language. All translations are, to a degree, interpretations, even when they aim to stay as close as possible to the original. The paraphrases that have appeared lately are nothing but interpretations with specific agendas. Following the example of professor Loasby, I have been meditating on Paul's letters with others looking over my shoulders. I offer to them my meditations hoping they consider them invitations to study his letters again.

Introduction

Since the rise of modern biblical scholarship there has not been unanimity as to how to characterize Paul. He has been praised for having delivered Christianity from Judaism. Lately it has been argued that he remained so thoroughly a Jew that he was not a Christian at all. Others think he became a Christian because he had become a totally frustrated Pharisee by his failure to observe the law of Moses. Some consider him to have been a male chauvinist with few redeeming qualities. Others see in him a messianist with masochistic tendencies. Some think he was a conceited authoritarian who had no patience with the views of others. For a time it was popular to see him as a mystic who wished to lose himself by being in Christ. It has been said that, as one concerned with the life of the Spirit, he saw reason as the enemy of faith and required his converts to sacrifice the intellect on the altar of submission to authority. All these are, at least in part, reactions against the prevailing picture of him as the one who laid the foundation for the doctrines of righteousness by faith and the God of grace on which the Protestant Reformation was built.

Friedrich Nietzsche considered Paul an ambitious and cunning authoritarian with delusions of grandeur and a lust for power, a very unpleasant and insecure man due to his anxiety as to how best to keep the Jewish law. He had come to see the law as the cross "to which he felt himself nailed." According to him, by becoming Christian, thanks to the apostleship of Paul, the radiant and healthy Greek culture of Apollo and Dionysus was subverted and almost lost, much to the detriment of Western culture.

As early as the Middle Ages Paul was seen as one who denied the life of the senses, especially what had to do with sexuality. He was paraded as the model celibate, an other-worldly idealist. Back then his other-worldliness and denial of the life of the senses was considered positively. Today these attributes are counted against him. It is somewhat of a surprise to find that one of the Church Fathers of the second century saw him as the apostle of the heretics. Still, even those who highlight negative aspects of his ministry find it impossible to dismiss him all together. He was, no doubt, a powerful personality who incited strong reactions during his lifetime and ever since.

Today most scholars would say that Paul was not a doctrinal builder. It has also become more difficult to see him as a mystic who wished to escape from the troubles and conflicts of life in this world. My reading of Paul tells me that he was very much in touch with the human reality, and understood that faith and reason are inseparable faculties of the healthy Christian. My meditations on his letters tell me that he was very much a Jew of the first century, fully conversant with Hellenistic culture and totally committed to faith in the God of his fathers.

As one wishing to understand the thought of the apostle Paul, my first task must be to consider the evidence now available for determining the sources of his thought. It is quite legitimate to take for granted the traditional assignments of authorship and to read Paul's letters for devotional purposes. It is possible to write a systematic presentation of the canonical Paul by extracting elements from all the letters ascribed to him according to the traditional rubrics of systematic theology. Such volumes quite often say more about their authors than about Paul. If, on the other hand, one's purpose is to come to terms with Paul's Gospel in his own time and culture and evaluate his role as a participant in the formation of what eventually became Christianity, then one must do a thorough analysis of the letters traditionally considered his and come to some conclusions concerning their authorship.

The New Testament canon contains thirteen letters which claim to have been written by Paul and one that has traditionally been ascribed to him. With the rise of modern literary and historical criticism, the authorship of these letters has come under scrutiny, and the Pauline authorship of some of them has been denied by many scholars. Today every student of Paul agrees that Paul wrote seven letters. These are: *To the Romans, To the Corinthians I, To the Corinthians II, To the Galatians, To the Philippians, To the Thessalonians I* and *To Philemon*. The Pauline authorship of the other seven is defended by some scholars and denied by others. Each one of these, of course, is considered separately and judged differently as to its claims to Pauline authorship.

Already by the time of the Renaissance the Pauline authorship of *To the Hebrews*, which does not claim to have been written by Paul, was being questioned by biblical students. Today most scholars do not think that Paul wrote it. The evidence against its Pauline authorship is overwhelming, both in terms of style and of content. In terms of style, its Greek is, together with that of Luke and Acts, the most stylish of the New Testament, a much higher literary Greek than that of the letters of Paul. Its rhetorical format, as an extended exhortation to Christians who seem to be getting tired of the demands the gospel makes on them, and are discouraged by their failings along the way, indicates that it does not belong to the early stages of the Christian mission. In terms of content, its vocabulary is quite distinct. It is preoccupied with the question of repentance, which is not a Pauline issue, and looks at sin primarily in cultic terms. Most significantly, its cosmology is cast in a Stoic symbolic universe, rather than the Platonic one found in Paul.

After *To the Hebrews* the letter *To the Ephesians* is probably the one whose Pauline authorship is denied by most scholars. Again, it is a matter of its style and content. Both argue for its belonging to the latter part of the first century. It has been said that in the letters of Paul the arguments move like a mountain brook, jumping and bubbling in a rapid flow. By contrast, in Ephesians the presentation moves ponderously and slowly like a river in a plain. The sentences are extremely long with numerous dependent clauses and repetitive grandeur. It represents the beginnings of liturgical pomposity.

The content of *To the Ephesians* also differs significantly with that of Paul's writings. Rather than to have the future *Parousia* (the public appearance of an enthroned Christ) as its focus, it is satisfied with life within the church built on the foundation of the apostles. Paul would never agree to a foundation other than Christ. For him, the apostles are only slaves of Christ. The purpose of the letter is to promote church unity. Thus, it evinces the transition of Christianity from a movement to an ecclesiastical phenomenon.

The Pastoral Epistles, *To Timothy I, To Timothy II* and *To Titus*, also belong to the same period and represent the beginnings of an ecclesiastical institution with hierarchical officials. Even if their style is more like that of Paul, the content deals with situations quite unknown at the time of Paul. In Paul's time, Christianity was not yet firmly distinguished from Judaism, and women were quite prominent in the leadership of the house churches.

To the Thessalonians II is considered by many to have been written by someone other than Paul primarily because of its view of the *Parousia*. While in *To the Thessalonians I* the *Parousia* is expected to take place momentarily, certainly when both Paul and the addressees are still alive, in *To the Thessalonians II* the emphasis is a warning against expecting that the *Parousia* will take place any time soon. Also the tone of these letters is quite different. While in the first Paul addresses the Thessalonians in the most tender and familiar terms, picturing himself as both their mother and their father, in the second the author uses rather stern imposing language.

The letter on which the scholarly opinion is most balanced between those in favor and those opposed to its having been written by Paul is *To the Colossians*. I agree with those who conclude that it was not written by Paul. My reasons are quite simple. In the first place, the letter is an argument against those teachers who make Christianity a kind of mystery cult in which, by means of ascetic practices that follow prescribed rules and regulations, individuals ascend to the heavenly spheres ruled by the "elemental spirits of the world" and participate in worship with angels. In other words, it has to do with the need to attain to perfection by self-denial in order to travel through the spheres. As most students recognize, the subject matter is somewhat similar to that which Paul deals with in

To the Galatians, which also refers to the "elemental spirits of the world" in reference to "works of law" (Gal. 3:14; 4:3). Dealing with this question in *To the Galatians* Paul enters into a full discussion of the nature and the function of Torah, the law, in order to show the error of those teaching that such endeavors are necessary. In the letter *To the Colossians* there is not one single allusion, much less a reference to Torah. The argument is based on the wording of an early Christian hymn instead. Besides, circumcision, the identity mark of Judaism which is repeatedly relativized by Paul in *To the Galatians*, *To the Romans*, and *To the Corinthians I*, plays a central role as a metaphor for the crucifixion in *To the Colossians*. The death of Christ on the cross, rather than being the death of the humanity descended from Adam, is the circumcision that perfects the body of the universe, which is, in fact, the body of Christ. In turn the baptism of Christians is the circumcision that perfects them. In Paul's letters the body of Christ is not the Pleroma, the fullness of all things in the universe, but the community of those baptized into his death and resurrection. Paul's vision is sociological and historical, while the universe of *To the Colossians* is esoteric and cosmic.

It must be recognized, of course, that the judgment that a particular book of the New Testament was not written by Paul does not in any way reflect on its canonical authority or its inspiration. Not all the books of the New Testament were written by Paul, of course, and we do not know the identity of the writers of many of the biblical books, most significantly of the authors of the four gospels. The issue here is determining which books may be used to paint a picture of the thought of Paul.

Those who use all of the fourteen books ascribed to Paul as evidence for a presentation of Paul's thought, defend their position by arguing that with the passage of time Paul grew in understanding and thus his thought evolved with experience and maturation. It is absolutely true that we all grow and mature in our thinking and that we do not necessarily see things in the same way when we are twenty and when we are sixty years old. In the case of Paul, however, two things militate against the view that his writings reflect maturation and growth with experience. One is that the ministry of Paul did not last forty years. His first letter is usually dated around the year 50 CE, and he died around the year 62 CE, thus his writings come from a twelve year period of his life. The other is that the evidence I have outlined above does not show development, but at best significant differences and at worst contradictions.

On the basis of the above considerations, my meditations will draw from the seven letters I am confident came from him. Of course, most probably Paul did not actually write any of them. His practice was to dictate them to one of his associates. At the end of *To the Romans*, Tertius, "the writer of this letter" (Rom. 16:22), sends greetings to the addressees. At the conclusion of *To the Corinthians I*, we read: "I, Paul, write this greeting with my own hand" (1 Cor. 16:21). Apparently, this endorsement came to be used by those who wrote pseudonymously. The sentence appears at the end of *To the Colossians* and of *To the Thessalonians II*. In the latter case, it adds: "This is the mark in every letter of mine; It is the way I write" (Col. 4:18; 2 Th. 3:17). If that were true, with the exception of *To the Corinthians I*, none of his actual letters were written by him. *To the Galatians* is without a doubt the letter which Paul wrote in a state of extreme agitation. Apparently, after having dictated the body of the letter, he took the stylus and the papyrus from the scribe and wrote himself 6:11 – 18, giving a concise summary of his gospel as the proclamation of a new creation and ending with a rather abrupt dismissal of his opponents. This section begins with the words, "See with what large letters I am writing to you with my own hand." Apparently Paul's calligraphy was not up to par.

Another important factor to be taken into account is that we do not possess any of the original letters. The earliest manuscripts in our possession come from the latter part of the second century, and they are only fragments of letters. We have full texts from the middle of the third century on. Besides, the letters were sent to different churches. After having been read at their meeting, they were stored we know not where or how. At the time Paul was not considered a prominent Christian personality, and it is clear that some of the letters evoked strong negative reactions. Certainly Paul wrote letters that were lost in antiquity. In *To the Corinthians I,* he refers to a letter written to the Corinthians sometime before (1 Cor. 5:9).

Most likely, what brought Paul to the attention of Early Christianity was the publication of *Acts of the Apostles,* where Paul is presented as the thirteenth disciple and the pioneer of the mission to the Gentiles. Whoever took it upon himself to collect and publish his letters sometime after that, remains unknown. The collector and publisher missed some letters and edited fragments of letter as a single letter. Thus, *To the Corinthians II* consists of several fragments that have been pieced together. The same may be the case of *To the Philippians,* which seems to consist of two fragments. Scholars also consider possible that whoever collected and published the letters, or another hand, may have added a phrase or two here and there. While I recognize that we have letters that went through a process of collecting and editing some thirty years after they were written, my purpose is not to reconstruct their history but to understand the thought of Paul through them. Still, in my meditations I will take into account the possibility of additions to the authentic letters by a later hand. These factors do not in the least diminish my admiration and respect for Paul as I endeavor to put the results of my struggles with them into clear, comprehensible, simple, language.

In my meditations I had to bridge three gaps: the language gap, the culture gap, and the time gap. In the first place there is a language gap. It becomes quite evident, for example, when considering the words "faith" and "beliefs." These English words are sometimes used synonymously and at others a differentiation is made between having faith and having beliefs. Beside, in English there is no verbal form of the noun "faith." In Greek, the root *pist* is used for the verb *pisteuo* and the noun *pistis.* Something is lost when "having faith" [*pisteuo*] becomes "believing." The action takes a purely intellectual connotation. Examples of this kind can be easily found. Something is lost when the Greek *diakonia* becomes "dispensation," or *psyxe* is translated "mind."

The second is a culture gap. These days our culture is becoming more aware of our holistic nature. It is readily recognized, for example, that there are psycho-somatic disorders, that one cannot treat the body as if it were a machine. Still, there are strong forces in the culture eager to deny the existence of the soul and to reduce reality to its material manifestations. Matters of the mind and the soul, both reasoning processes and emotional reactions are considered just electrical and chemical phenomena in the brain. Some claim that all that is can be explained by science. Our secularized culture is quite different from the Hellenistic culture in which Paul lived and preached the Gospel. While philosophers had been for some time making a critical evaluation of the pervasive mythologies that informed everyday life, most of the people lived in a world in which the human and the divine worlds were mutually permeable.

Even though our culture of late is recognizing that we are social beings, we Westerners still live in individualistic societies. This means that we tend to interpret Paul in individualistic and dualistic terms. Paul, however, took human beings to be integrated units of body, soul and spirit; but each unit was a member of a corporate personality. In this, he was quite true to his Hebraic traditions.

As a good apocalypticist he affirmed the reality of the Fall that introduced evil into the world. It placed the world under the power of sin and "the god of this world." Even if apocalypticism is now quite popular as a format for entertainment, it is not taken seriously in our scientific culture. This means that if the faith of Paul is to be taken seriously, his expression of it in apocalyptic terms must be transcribed into meaningful contemporary cultural terms. In these meditations I limit myself to bridging the cultural gap to make the message of Paul understandable in Paul's own terms within his symbolic universe. I will not elaborate how his message may best be expressed in the twenty first century.

The time gap has two dimensions. In the first place, between us and Paul there are twenty centuries of human history, and one must make every effort not to be anachronistic. Besides there is a most important difference in the way in which we place ourselves in time. Paul, no doubt, understood himself to be living in the time when the *Parousia* of the Lord was to take place momentarily. We live two thousand years later and the *Parousia* has not taken place. Today it is impossible to announce an imminent *Parousia* and be credible outside the apocalyptic mindset. Again, my conscious effort is to make Paul's understanding of time an important factor to be taken into account when reading him. I leave it to my readers to find in Paul's faith a meaningful way to understand themselves in time once most people cannot envision its imminent end by the hand of God. Besides, with the coming of the atomic age, humans have demonstrated their capacity to destroy the world without God's help. Thank you very much, God; but, no thanks. This gives a totally different perspective to our understanding of ourselves in space and time.

The letters make clear that Paul had a strong personality and a quick temper. He could flare up and issue anathemas as well as become contrite and appeal for understanding in the sweetest terms. They also reveal that he was not one of the leaders of the church, and did not enjoy wide acceptance during his lifetime. Envoys sent by the leaders in Jerusalem seem to have trailed him trying to undo what Paul had been doing. Paul admits that in the sight of others he made an unimpressive appearance. *The Acts of Paul and Thecla*, a second century legend, gives an admiring but not idealistic picture of him. "In stature he was a man of middling size, and his hair was scanty, and his legs were a little crooked, and his knees were projecting, and he had large [another version, "blue"] eyes, and his eyebrows met, and his nose was somewhat long, and he was full of grace and mercy; at one time he seemed like a man, and at another time he seemed like an angel." The many details would argue that this straightforward description preserves something of a living tradition concerning Paul's physical appearance.

Whatever his appearance may have been, no doubt, he was an amazing human being who took it upon himself to carry in his flesh the marks of Jesus (Gal. 6:17). It is also quite evident that he lived in the real world of human struggles and personality conflicts, His correspondence with the Corinthians reveals the serious tensions that developed between them and Paul. He refers to having made them a visit that resulted in a total break up of their relationship (2 Cor. 2:1). The catalogue of the many punishments he suffered while engaged in his service of Christ leaves no doubt of the reality of the world in which he lived (2 Cor. 11:23 – 28). He faced squarely the present, rather than escaping to the past or the future. It is because of this, that I find his writings extremely relevant.

My admiration of Paul does not mean that I do not read his letters critically, that is to say, seriously, or that I take everything he says as normative. I like to meditate on his letters to internalize how he lived his Christianity in the first century so as to live my Christianity well in the twenty first. I take very seriously his faith and I share it. How he expressed his faith in his time and culture gives me models with which to express my faith in my time and culture.

No doubt Martin Luther read Paul in a new way and did a great service to the future of the Gospel. His struggles with the entrenched theology of his day liberated many from the non-gospel of guilt and punishments predominant in his day. The battles Luther fought, however, need be fought no longer. Righteousness by Faith and *Sola Scriptura* have become common currency in the Christian landscape. God's grace is now preached from every pulpit; Catholics have become as serious students of the Bible as any Protestant, and Protestants have become aware of the importance of Tradition as much as Catholics have long been. It is high time, therefore, to outgrow the tensions that separated Christians after Luther. Reading Paul with Righteousness by Faith and *Sola Scriptura* as determining factors can only prevent the reading of Paul on his own terms. The problem these days is, to a large degree, that Righteousness by Faith and *Sola Scriptura* have become slogans for modern ideological distortions of the Gospel.

Today many Christians read the Bible overlooking the actual authors of the different books, pretending that the Bible has only one author. This is a willful failure to look at the evidence. I think that the richness of the Bible can only be tapped when each one of its authors is given the opportunity to speak authentically in time and space. It is when Paul is allowed to be Paul that one gains a sense of his flaming faith, hope and love. When a biblical author becomes a real person expressing faith under inspiration, what is read takes on new meaning and authority. The message is more authentic when the human factor is given its due. I trust my readers will find in these meditations invitations to have profitable dialogues with Paul.

I  My Gospel

It is difficult to know how the disciples of Jesus, immediately after the crucifixion and the appearances of the Risen Lord, understood what had taken place among them during the last year and a half. Our first documents are the letters of Paul and the first among them is usually dated around the year 50 CE. The oral traditions that circulated during the twenty years between the crucifixion and the first letter of Paul eventually found their way into the written gospels. Since each one of them gives a peculiar voice and agenda to the teachings of Jesus it is not easy to distinguish what Jesus actually taught and what the Christians made of his teachings by the time the gospels were written. In any case, it is quite clear that the Gospel preached by Paul was a very radical interpretation of the crucifixion and the resurrection of Jesus Christ.

Most notable in this regard is that Paul hardly refers to the teachings of Jesus. To Paul what counts is that God had revealed His righteousness. That is to say, God had achieved a significant part of the purpose for which He had created the human family. Of course, the only way to know about God's efforts to achieve the purpose of creation is by knowing the Scriptures that tell of the dealings of God with the Israelites. They tell of the many ways in which in the past God's purposes had been frustrated by the rebellions and the intransigence of the Israelites. They also record, however, the promises God made and the praises with which the people glorified their God on account of His fulfillment of the promises.

To come to terms with Paul's Gospel it is essential to recognize that Paul is concerned with an existential problem. Anyone who looks at what takes place in the affairs of men and women in the world has great difficulty finding manifestations of the righteousness of God. This was already the case at the time of the exile of the Jews in Babylon. The prophets had been proclaiming the gospel of God's retributive justice. Those who do good are rewarded for their goodness and those who do evil are punished on account of their evil deeds. Looking at what was happening when Jerusalem was destroyed by the Babylonians and the Israelites were in exile in Mesopotamia, the prophet Habakkuk understandably found the situation confusing. That the Israelites should be punished for their sins was taken for granted. Their exile was, therefore, quite understandable. That the Babylonians, a people who were famous for their cruelty, were being rewarded by giving them the spoils of Jerusalem and its wealth was totally incomprehensible. Habakkuk was therefore quite confused and asked the obvious question. Where is God's justice to be seen?

The atmosphere that gave rise to Habakkuk's question was the incubator that gave birth to a new understanding of history. The Hebrew prophets were the first to find meaning in life by looking at it in terms of its development in time, rather than its moorings in nature. This gives them the honor of having been the ones who discovered that history, rather than nature, provides the scenario where human life is to be understood. According to the prophets, God guides the affairs not only of the people with whom He had made a covenant but also of the other nations. For Israel to be prosperous and happy it had to demonstrate covenant loyalty. As long as experience confirmed that the righteous prosper and the wicked suffer, life in God's world made sense. If, on the other hand, the wicked prosper and the righteous suffer, life ceased to make sense. The fact that history contained ample evidence that the righteous suffer and the wicked prosper gave rise to new developments in theology.

Among the Israelites these developments took two basic forms. One was the Wisdom movement among the cosmopolitan elites who were quite aware of the cultural currents of the Mediterranean world. It answered Habakkuk's question by establishing a great gulf separating God from humankind. This was informed by the philosophical awakening taking place in Greece. Notions of God as if he were a man with the same desires, passions and virtues were thoroughly critiqued and abandoned by the emerging Hellenistic intellectuals. Among them it could no longer be argued that human beings were capable of understanding God's ways. Thus, the wise men of Israel distanced themselves from the prophetic understanding that human history is God's handiwork. God's activity is beyond any human capacity to understand. That is the message of the books of Job and Ecclesiastes.

The other attempt to answer Habakkuk's question brought about the development of a new way to understand history, that is, by the *apocalyptic* twist to the prophetic movement. The transformation of the prophetic view of history into its apocalyptic step child took some time developing. The prophetic conception of history took the cyclical view of time, prevalent in societies bound to the celebration of feasts attached to a yearly routine, and opened it into a linear time-line extending to an open future. This had been a radical departure from the understanding of time as an unending annual return to the beginning accompanied by the repetition of the human labors that pertain to the seasons that are marked by the solar and lunar movements. The prophets pointed to the future Day of the Lord, when God's retributive justice would have its ultimate manifestation. According to them, the Day of the Lord would be a day in history. In that future day God would gather all the nations and establish Himself as King in Jerusalem.

The apocalypticists, on the other hand, bent the prophetic time line back to the beginning, and conceived the Day of the Lord as the day in which history came to an end, making room for a new beginning. Instead of a yearly cycle, the apocalypticists made a cycle of the whole of human history. The destruction of historical time was necessitated, they asserted, by the enormity of present evil. History could not be repaired by the establishment of God's throne in Jerusalem as the prophets had predicted. It required a more radical solution, a return to a totally new beginning.

Apocalypticism answered Habakkuk's question relying on the doctrine of the resurrection with which the Israelites had become acquainted during their contact with Zoroastrianism in Babylon. God's retributive justice is not in evidence in this life. It will be operative in the life to come. It is possible to maintain that God's retributive justice works when rewards and punishments are given in an afterlife, after the dead are raised from their tombs. Thus, in spite of the fact that in this life the just may unjustly suffer, they will receive their just reward at their resurrection when God establishes a new beginning.

In the process of finding an answer to Habakkuk's question which affirmed God's retributive justice, apocalyptic visionaries came to a new understanding of the world in which humans live. Instead of the world created by God which, according to Genesis 1, God had declared good in every way, and which, as the prophets said, was under God's direct control, apocalypticists saw the world corrupted and no longer under God's direct control. They introduced the doctrine of the Fall of creation. On account of the sin of Adam and Eve, the whole of creation has fallen into corruption and is under the power of "the rulers of this world," Satan and his evil angels. The expulsion of Adam and Eve from the garden of Eden was not just a historical event in the life of the first couple. It was a cosmic event with universal consequences. It placed the whole of creation under the power of Satan, "the god of this world."

This new theology developed at a time when the conquests of Alexander the Great propagated Greek culture in the Near East. Greek philosophers had questioned anthropomorphic understandings of the gods and had relegated the order of the divine to regions that were beyond human reach. These developments also influenced the Wisdom movement in Israel, as noted above. The separation of the human and the divine that had been developed within Hellenism, and which was used differently within different thought currents, was conceived by apocalypticism as the space occupied by the fallen angels and their leader. From the heavenly spheres they exercised their evil influence on humanity. This made it possible to affirm that the evil amply evident in the world is due to the fallen state in which God's creation is now found. Under Satan's direct control, creation has been corrupted. The world is under the power of evil.

The preponderance of evil in the world is what necessitates the destruction of the present fallen world before humans may live in a good world. On the Day of the Lord not even God will be able to repair the damage caused by Satan and his angels. God will destroy His creation and start all over with a New Heaven and a New Earth. This new beginning gave the apocalyptic visionaries the opportunity to retrieve the language of the ancient myths of creation in which battles between heavenly beings are waged in order to destroy the forces of evil and make possible the creation of a good world for humans to inhabit. Descriptions of the Day of the Lord in which goodness triumphs over evil and God's justice is vindicated gave apocalyptic visionaries ample room to expand their theological imaginations. The descriptions that have come down to us are quite varied and testify to their appeal. Still, most of them have at their core the notion of the Two Ages: This Present Evil Age and The Age to Come.

The difference between the two ages is like night and day. Contrasting them became a major undertaking in Pharisaism and in Rabbinic Judaism. Such a radical transformation of reality could not possibly be accomplished in one day. As a consequence, the Age of Messiah was introduced into this scheme, a time in which the details of this transition could be accomplished. One of the main events in the Age of Messiah would be the resurrection of the just so that they could receive their reward, and demonstrate that God's retributive justice works. The conception of Messiah, however, was not firmly established. Messiah means "anointed," and in Israel persons had been anointed for different functions. Judges were anointed with the spirit to become military liberators from oppressive neighbors (Philistines, Canaanites, Ammonites, etc.). Kings were anointed to rule over Jerusalem. Priests were anointed to serve at the Tabernacle in the desert or the temple in Jerusalem, Prophets were given "a word of the Lord." All these figures provided models for the descriptions of the coming Messiah who would establish the Age to Come, a totally new reality for the just to live in. At the time of Jesus and Paul, Pharisees, Covenanters of Qumran (the people of the Dead Sea Scrolls), Zealots and others shared apocalyptic visions of the future Age to Come where God's retributive justice would ultimately be revealed.

Whether Jesus shared the apocalyptic world view of many of his contemporaries is a matter much debated by modern scholars. Most scholars today think that Paul lived in an apocalyptic symbolic universe, and I share this opinion. The only way to understand him is by recognizing the apocalyptic framework of his exposition of the Gospel. In this connection it is important to bear in mind that there was no standard apocalyptic vision maintained by a recognized theological authority. On account of this, some scholars refrain from using the noun apocalypticism and use only the adjective apocalyptic. I will use both the noun and the adjective to refer to the broad theological movement that is characterized by solving the problem of God's justice in the world by means of the doctrines of the Fall, the resurrection, and the Two Ages.

Paul found meaning for the crucifixion and the resurrection of Christ in the basic apocalyptic framework of the Fallen Creation, the Age of Messiah and the Age to Come. For him the Good News was that the crucifixion of Jesus had put an end to the dominion of Satan on the Fallen Creation, and the resurrection of Christ had established the Age of Messiah as the New Creation. Any day soon the Age to Come would displace the Age of Messiah. The Gospel is that God has revealed his justice by establishing the order of life in the Spirit, or life in Christ, by raising the crucified Jesus by the power of the Spirit, thereby breaking the power of Satan within the Present Age. In other words, the Gospel announces that it is possible to be free from the powers that rule the Fallen Creation, even while living in bodies of flesh, that is to say, in the natural world. Paul's Gospel affirms that God's justice has been revealed in the death and the resurrection of His Son. The Day of the Lord, when God acts on behalf of the just and makes all things right, has come.

The establishment of a new creation by raising the Lord Jesus from the dead is the powerful demonstration of the justice of God. As Paul sees it, the Gospel is not primarily concerned with Jesus, his life, his activities, his teachings. The Gospel is, rather, the demonstration of the power and justice of God. Proclamation or announcement by itself is not quite Gospel. What makes the proclamation Gospel is what God accomplishes in people. The Gospel is the power of the Spirit at work in the resurrection of Christ and in the giving of life to those who believe in the God who raised Christ, thus making it possible for them to live "in the Spirit," that is, by the power of the Spirit that raised Christ from the dead.

Paul refers to the Gospel he preaches as "God's gospel" (2 Co. 11:7) and as "the gospel of Christ" (2 Cor. 2:12), or the "gospel of his [God's] Son" (Rom. 1:9). He also characterizes it as "my gospel" (Rom. 2:16; 16:25), or, since he is very aware of his co-workers, as "our gospel" (2 Cor. 4:3; 1 Th. 1:5). As an apostle sent to preach the Gospel Paul often found himself defending his mission from various charges (2 Cor. 3:1; 7:2; 11:5 – 7; Gal. 1:10). Doing so at times he wonders whether he is inappropriately boasting, making too high a claim for himself. On these occasions he always makes the point that the high claims are for the Gospel, not for himself as a minister of the Gospel. Probably the most extensive of these asides is found in chapters 3 and 4 of *To the Corinthians II*.

His argument gets a bit confusing at times, but as a whole it is quite effective. Recognizing that his understanding of the Gospel is not that of most other preachers of Christ, he refers to other gospels (Gal. 1:6, 9, 11; 2 Cor. 11:4) which he considers not to be gospels at all. To highlight his Gospel, he contrasts his function as an agent of the Gospel with that of Moses as the agent of the law given at Sinai. He begins his *de minoris ad maiorem* argument recognizing that the ministry, or service (*diakonía*) of Moses was accompanied with a glory that reflected itself with splendor in his face. Then he characterizes the content of Moses' ministry. His was a "dispensation of death." Paul consistently points out that the function of the law is to express the wrath of God that brings about condemnation and issues in death (Rom. 4:15). Having established this foundation, he brings about the logical conclusion: "if the dispensation of death. . . came with such splendor . . . will not the dispensation of the Spirit be attended with greater splendor?" The question is purely rhetorical. Paul then affirms the obvious: "For if there was splendor in the dispensation of condemnation, the dispensation of righteousness must far exceed it in splendor."

Having established the superior splendor of the dispensation of righteousness, Paul elaborates on the fact that the splendor in the face of Moses slowly faded away after he came down from Mt. Sinai. Since the splendor in Moses' face went away already during his lifetime, it follows that "what once had splendor has come to have no splendor at all, because of the splendor that surpasses it." That is to say, the splendor of the resurrection of Christ totally outshines whatever splendor was exhibited at Sinai. This gives rise to another observation: what once had splendor and now has no splendor at all was temporary. The splendor that now surpasses it is permanent. In other words, while the dispensation of death introduced by Moses' giving of the law was temporary, the dispensation of righteousness introduced by the Spirit that raised Christ from the dead is permanent.

Paul is now ready to make a point about another one of the elements in the story of the giving of the law at Mt. Sinai. He does it by elaborating creatively on the report that the splendor in Moses' face faded away. According to the story in Exodus 34:29 – 35, Moses put a veil on his face because the splendor in his face put fear in the hearts of the people. Eventually, once the splendor had faded away, the veil was no longer needed. Paul, however, says that Moses put a veil on his face in order to hide the fact that the splendor of his face was fading away. Then, he gives the story a surprising contemporary application. The veil in Moses' face, placed in order to hide its fading splendor, is now in the face of Paul's contemporaries who read "the old covenant" with hardened minds. Their veils prevent them "from seeing the light of the gospel of the glory of Christ, who is the likeness of God." In this way Paul explains why the gospel of the power of the Spirit that gives life to those who believe is not at work in those who preach a gospel based on the law.

Having pointed out its superior splendor and permanence, Paul establishes the authenticity of the Gospel of "the dispensation of the Spirit" of which he is a minister. It is the Gospel of "a new covenant" which brings about "righteousness." In other words, it establishes the righteousness of God since it manifests the purpose of creation. The law may have served to condemn and to bring about death. The righteousness of God is about life. The dispensation of the Spirit that gives life is then given its ultimate definition: "The Lord is the Spirit, and where the Spirit of the Lord is, there is freedom. And we all, with unveiled face, beholding the glory of the Lord, are being changed into his likeness from one degree of glory to another; for this comes from the Lord who is the Spirit." The contrasts have reached their intended goal. The glory in the face of Moses was transitory. The veil in the face of Moses is now in the face of the people who read the Old Testament with hardened minds. The veil, however, can be taken away by Christ. In the dispensation of the Spirit the glory of the Risen Christ is permanent, and is seen by those whose faces have been unveiled. His glory is being reflected in the faces of those who have the freedom to see it. Those from whose faces Christ has taken away the veil and read the "old covenant" correctly not only can behold the glory in Christ's face. They are being changed by participating in Christ's glory into ever higher degrees of glory until they finally receive their spiritual, glorious bodies at the resurrection of the dead (1 Cor. 15:44).

Ultimately, the truth of the Gospel, according to Paul, is its power to bring about the unveiling of the mind and the freedom to see the Gospel of the glory of the Risen Christ and be changed from one degree of glory to another. Paul concludes his argument with the clarification. "We have this treasure [the Gospel] in earthen vessels, to show that the transcendent power belongs to God and not to us." Thus, even though he has audaciously compared his role as an apostle of the Gospel of the Risen Christ with the role of Moses as the agent of the law at Sinai, Paul ends up clarifying that what is at stake is not his ministry. It is the righteousness of God. The transcendent power that brought the crucified and buried Jesus to a new glorious life by the Spirit is at the center of his Gospel. "The word of the cross" which most consider nonsense, Paul confesses that to the believers "who are being saved it is the power of God" (1 Cor. 1:18). Paul then encapsulates his view in an epigram: the Gospel of "the kingdom of God does not consist in talk but in power" (1 Cor. 4:20). The same is true of the Gospel.

As said above, Paul understands the significance of the Gospel within an apocalyptic framework. It serves to reveal that, after all, retributive justice works. People will receive what they deserve. On that account, Paul points out that "our gospel is veiled . . . to those who are perishing." In their case the god of this world has blinded the minds of the unbelievers to keep them from seeing the light of the gospel of the glory of Christ. The preaching of the Gospel may bring about "the freedom to see" to those who with unveiled faces see the glory of the Risen Lord, but it may also bring about "perishing" to those who, on account of the blindness of their minds, with veiled faces fail to experience the transcendent power of the Gospel.

As an apocalyptic thinker Paul does not elaborate the power of God in cosmic battles with the forces of the god of this world. He does not give descriptions of the stages in the war between good and evil popular in apocalyptic writings. The power of God that reveals His righteousness has already been demonstrated at the resurrection of Christ. Now in his spirit body the glory of Christ is permanent, and the power that brought about that glorious resurrection is actively bringing about changes from glory to glory in those who with unveiled faces have the freedom to behold the glory of the Lord. To those who thought that Paul, as a well-trained Pharisee, should be ashamed of preaching a gospel that viewed the revelation of God at Sinai as one which, even though resplendent with glory at the time, was temporary and had now been superseded by the revelation of the power of the Spirit that raised Christ from the dead, Paul replied, "I am not ashamed of the gospel. It is the power of God for salvation to everyone who has faith" (Rom. 1:16). Reminding the Thessalonians of the time when he first preached to them, Paul writes, "our gospel came to you not only in word, but also in power and in the Holy Spirit and in full conviction" (1 Th. 1:5). The power of the Holy Spirit that brings about the full conviction that changes lives is what really counts.

The gospel is not primarily concerned with a message. It is about the power of God that gives freedom and changes lives even now, and into the future. Writing to the Corinthians, who apparently were having second thoughts about the Gospel he had preached to them, Paul challenges their argument that the Gospel of the cross lacks wisdom. He reminds them of the time when he had been with them, saying "my speech and my message were not in plausible words of wisdom, but in demonstrations of the Spirit and power, that your faith might not rest in the wisdom of men but in the power of God" (1 Cor. 2:4 – 5). Paul understands that true faith cannot rest in the words of a human agent. Essentially, the Gospel is not wisdom as it is commonly understood. The faith that counts rests on the power of God to be righteous. The changes in the lives of those who have experienced the power of God are then reflected in the way in which believers conduct themselves in society. Writing to the Philippians, Paul advices them, "Only let your manner of life be worthy of the gospel of Christ" (Phil. 1:27). They are not being asked to give a worthy intellectual account of the gospel with cogent arguments and valid biblical foundations. The power of the gospel changes lives. Christians are expected to have a manner of life in society that reflects the splendor of the Risen Christ. That is the triumph of righteousness over sin that Paul, the peculiar apocalypticist, is primarily concerned with.

The author of *To the Hebrews* gives a magnificent description of the glory and the power demonstrated by God at Sinai — glory that brightened the skies with lightning and power that made the mountain shake. He finds in that event the precedent of what will take place at the future manifestation of glory and power when the present shakable creation is to be dismantled and the unshakable, eternal world is established with the heavenly Jerusalem on Mt. Zion (Heb. 12:18 – 28). Like the author of *To the Hebrews*, Paul refers to the glory and the power accompanying the giving of the law at Sinai. For him, however, the ultimate manifestation of God's "transcendent power" (2 Cor. 4:7) has already taken place at the resurrection of Christ. The light shining on the face of the Risen Christ is the light that drove away the darkness "at the beginning." The glory and the power that brought about the life of both the First Adam and the Last Adam now gives life to humans still living in the flesh and changes them from glory to glory till they attain to the glorious spiritual body at their resurrection from the dead. That is Paul's Gospel.

II FAITH, HOPE AND LOVE

Modern scholarship has been debating for some time whether Paul was primarily a theologian or an ethicist. What was his primary interest when he wrote his letters? Was it to announce what God had done, or to point out how Christians should live? His letters usually begin with theological expositions and end with ethical admonitions. Did he write the first to establish the basis for the second, or did he write the second as corollaries of the first? When he paced about the room dictating to a scribe, was he trying to argue or to advise? In some significant ways the answers to these questions determine how one interprets Paul.

It seems to me that these questions are poorly framed because for Paul it was not a matter of either/or, but of both/and. That is why he considered faith, hope and love a trilogy (1 Cor. 13:13). When he wrote about them in *To the Corinthians I*, for example, he was both arguing and advising. Faith and hope may be thought to be exercises of the mind, while love may seem to be more a matter of the heart. Paul regularly thinks of the three as an indivisible whole. He does not give priority to faith, but ends by saying that the greatest of the three is love. Love takes its place as a crowning or a fulfillment of the other two. Faith and hope, moreover, should not be considered separately, as having their fulfillment in themselves. Faith has been reduced at times to the ability to affirm a proposition. This is the case, for example, in the *Letter of James*. If faith is to affirm that "God is one," then the devils also have faith (Jas. 2:19). Hope, has been understood as expecting something without warrants. For Paul, Christian faith, hope and love are interlaced in a wonderful spiritual knot.

Since Paul's time, Christianity has been conceived by some as an idea, as a theological construct, as a system of doctrines, as something to be considered and approved intellectually, as a way of thinking with which one is in agreement and one has adopted as a guide. Paul insisted that Christianity is a way of being and living. For him, human beings are an integrated spirit, soul and body (1 Th. 5:23). These aspects of being cannot be separated. Humans are integrated wholes. Any one of these three words, spirit, soul, body, can be used to refer to the whole person.

The mind does not operate in a vacuum. As it operates it expresses itself in a concrete environment through the body. Faith and hope may be thought as purely intellectual activities — but Paul says "Not quite!" Christian faith and hope cannot be apart from love because in such case they would lack accountability. Indeed, faith and hope are possible on account of God's love, and are effective when they manifest themselves as Christian love, which can only be a concrete expression of faith and hope. According to Paul, Christian faith, hope and love abide together. Thus, Christians don't live in the past affirming their faith in what God did in Christ, neither do they live daydreaming about the future final triumph of God's righteousness. They live in the present, loving the world by being engaged with it.

The crucifixion of Jesus in Judea under Roman imperial rule was an execution, and, if the accounts in the gospels are to be believed, all those who witnessed it saw it as such. The resurrection of Christ did not have witnesses. All we have to go by are the reports of people who saw him alive three days later and afterward. As a matter of fact, life in this world has not changed much on account of what some Roman soldiers did in the environs of Jerusalem, and historians have not considered the action of those soldiers worthy of mention in their accounts of the Roman Empire. Faith and hope, however, are built on what happened then, and they have changed the lives of believers since.

Only faith may affirm that God acted in Jesus' death and resurrection. Only faith can affirm that Jesus died "for our sins," as the earliest Christian confession declares (1 Cor. 15:3). For Paul, to have faith is to appropriate God's action in the past and make it one's own. Only then the purpose of Christ's incarnation becomes a reality in a human being. On the basis of faith a Christian can hope. The future offers hope to those who have internalized the cross and the resurrection of Christ. For Paul, hope presupposes faith. Faith has its object in the past. Hope has its object in the future. What one says about the future, if it is not going to prove a chimera, can only be affirmed with certainty on the basis of what the past has demonstrated about the one who promised what is hoped for. The Christian hope for life in the Age to Come can only be based on God's past action. Christians live on the basis of their faith in what God has done and their hope in what God promised to do. As far as Paul is concerned, what God did at the cross and the resurrection was the fulfillment of his promise to Abraham. A promise is always a past event. One may expect a promise, but one does not have a promise until one has faith in the one who promised. Faith sees the execution of Jesus and the encounters with the Risen Christ as the fulfillment of the promise to Abraham. That is the basis on which a Christian hopes for the fulfillment of the promise of the Day of Christ.

It is neither necessary nor healthy to live in the past or the future. Therefore, faith and hope by themselves are not enough. Life must be lived in the present. Faith, as said above, grasps God's action in the crucifixion and the resurrection, things that happened in the past. Hope, anticipates the future triumph of God at the appearance of Christ in glory to be seen by all. Christians, however, must live in the present. Here is where love comes in.

The word "love" has become an abused concept. One hears of the love of wisdom, the love of sexual passion and the love of chocolate. Paul views love quite differently; for him, the love of God is the energy source for all divine action. Christian love is the power that transposes faith and hope into objective acts with consequences in the concreteness of the present. A melody that has been transposed to a different key remains the same but carries its message in a different mold. Christians must transpose their faith and hope from an intellectual key into a practical key. That is how faith and hope become Christian love. The Christian manner of being and living actualizes in the present what faith affirms about the past and hope envisions for the future. Normally, humans live in chronological time: from the past, through the present and into the future. Believers live their Christianity from the internalization of the past and the future of God's actions into the present of their own activity. They live in the present manifesting God's actions in human acts of love. Thus the past and the future of God become real in the present. In this way God's love for the world is historically present.

The Christian life is not a way of escaping from the reality of life in the world, as some throughout history have presented it. Neither is it a way of following the ancient and presently-popular formula *carpe diem,* seize the day. This dictum advises to live the present as if there were no tomorrow: forget the past and its burdens and have no illusions about tomorrow and its accidents. That is, live today for what it may offer you in immediate satisfactions.

For Paul, life must be lived fully in the present, and the only way to do that is to be rooted in a solid past event and have a clear vision of what life is for. Only when the present is a living testimony of where life is rooted and what it is about does the present have any claim to transcendence. For Paul, Christians must testify to the love of God; but love is not an emotion, or a feeling, or a virtue. It is not something that exists as such and can be defined by itself. Love is the working out of faith and hope (Gal. 5:6). It is the Christian "manner of life" in the world (Phil. 1:27). Paul's theology is the theology of living the full life, that is the theology of faith, hope and love, and his ethic is the ethic of the love that embraces the world.

Naming the fruit of the Spirit, Paul lists love first (Gal. 5:22). When he gives concrete ethical advice to the Romans, he begins by saying: "Let love be genuine" (Rom. 12:9). A more literal translation of the original Greek would be: "Our love [must] not [be] hypocritical." The original assumes the verb "to be" and supplies the definite article to the noun. It is not just any kind of love that Paul has in mind. He is writing about "the love," that is, Christian love. What would make Christian love hypocritical? A love that is not the manifestation of God's activity in the world. What does Paul consider to be genuine Christian love? A love that expresses faith in Christ's cross and hopes for full participation in Christ's glorification by extending to others the benefits of being "beloved by God" (1 Th. 1:4).

The intellectualization of faith had overtaken some members of the Christian community in Corinth. They trusted in their knowledge of God in order to defend a particular way of life both in church and in society. They lived under the slogan "We have knowledge" (1 Cor. 8:1), and the corollary to that slogan was "all things are lawful" (1 Cor. 2:12; 10:23). Paul insists that faith is not a way of gaining access to esoteric knowledge. Those claiming to posses it may be "puffed up." To such he says, "but love builds up" (1 Cor. 8:1). With two conditional sentences he takes away all claims to perfect knowledge and affirms, instead, the efficacy of love. "If any one imagines that he knows something, he does not yet know as he ought to know. But if one loves God, one is known by him" (1 Cor. 8:2 – 3). Christians do not trust what they know. They trust the God who knows them.

For Paul, faith and hope in God is not what ultimately count. A Christian's participation in the life of the Spirit, which is life in God, is only made evident by the life of love that reveals God's knowledge of that individual. The theological affirmations and the religious claims of Christians are not ultimately tested by their logic or by appeals to a biblical quotation. They are tested by the way in which the Christians who make them live out their faith and hope through acts of love, by whether their manner of life is worthy of the gospel. Even while Paul gives an important role to thinking and speaking he does not understands Christianity as a way of thinking, a way of knowing, or even a way of believing. He encouraged his readers to think critically and be fully persuaded intellectually as to what is God's will (Rom. 14:5). But he does not think that Christianity is primarily a matter of knowledge. For Paul, Christianity is a way of being. That is why the famous Pauline poem to love ends with the admonition, "Pursue love" (1 Cor. 14:1). He further advises the Corinthians, "Let all that you do be done in love" (1 Cor. 16:14).

At the core of Paul's exposition of the superiority of love are found the words "love bears all things, believes all things, hopes all things, endures all things" (1 Cor. 13:7). At first glance these phrases would seem to espouse passive submission to the vicissitudes of life. The phrases, however, form a classic chiasmic parallelism, well known to Hebrew poets. The first two terms deal with the present — love bears and believes. The second two look to the future — love hopes and endures. The first and the last — bears and endures — share content, and the second and third — believes and hopes — are love's two companions. Together the four terms are interlocked to bring out the stability and purposefulness of love. Love is not shaky, love is not insecure, love is not passive, love does not settle down for the *status quo.*, love is not a receptacle for things as they are. Paul cannot be charged with an ethic of passivity. His is not the Stoic ethic of emotional detachment. For him, love is positive, love is inventive, love is full of surprises, love is full of miracles. Love does not bear, believe, hope and endure because it is stupid, gullible, unrealistic or submissive to the point of irresponsibility. Love bears, believes, hopes and endures because it is powerfully grounded on God and embraces life.

In all its manifestations Christian love is one and the same because it is grounded on the unity of life in the Spirit that pours God's love into human hearts (Rom. 5:6). The workings of love reveal that the vitality to live comes from a source which is not one's own. Christian lovers are driven by the desire of creatures to be reunited with the source of life. For this reason love can only be the living expression of faith and hope.

Meditations on the Letters of Paul

Paul repeatedly links faith and love as twins that operate together in the lives of Christians. He also refers to the trinity of faith, hope and love, not only in the hymn to love in *To the Corinthians I*, but also in 1 Thess. 1:3 and 5:9. That faith, hope and love work together in the Christian life is explicitly said in ringing declarative sentences which describe the reality in which Christians live. Describing the present, not the past nor the future, he shows how faith, hope and love work together. He writes, "Therefore, since we are justified by faith, we have peace with God through our Lord Jesus Christ . . . and we rejoice in our hope of sharing the glory of God. More than that we rejoice in our sufferings . . . because God's love has been poured into our hearts through the Holy Spirit which has been given to us" (Rom. 5:1 – 5). Here faith, hope and love are interlocked with peace, Christ, joy and the Holy Spirit.

There is no more concise statement of Paul's Gospel in his letters. Several nuances of this statement are worthy of notice. It is implicit that justification is accomplished by God on account of our faith in Him. Our hope is dependent on our faith in God. Most telling is that God does not only justify. He also pours love into human hearts. He does not give it counting the drops. He does not sprinkle it. He does not stingily let it flow. He prodigally pours love. The trinity of faith, hope and love corresponds to the trinity of God who justifies, Christ who gives peace, and the Holy Spirit who is the agent of love. As the text goes on to point out, all this could happen because "God shows his love for us in that while we were yet sinners, Christ died for us" (Rom. 5:8). Thus, it is the love of God that provides the object for the faith that brings about God's justification. In turn, faith also brings about hope, and together these two make the love of those who believe and hope effective in the world. Faith and hope may be thought of as faculties that give transcendence to a person, and in some ways that is the case. Still, when they energize the love manifested by a person's actions, they actualize themselves in a most immanent way.

It is somewhat surprising to realize that Paul does not urge his converts to love God. He urges them to believe in, to obey, to fear, to know, to wait for, to trust in, to pray to God, but not to love God. There is just one possible exception, which is not a demand but a description, "We know that in everything God works for good with those who love him" (Rom. 8:28). This may be because he realized that love cannot be mandated. Christian love is not the result of a human's initiative. It is the response to God's initiative.

Paul's ethic of love is geared to the principle that it is impossible for love to wrong a neighbor (Rom. 13:10). When love controls conduct, the neighbor "for whom Christ died" (Rom. 14; 15; 1 Cor. 8:11) is to be prized accordingly. To act contrary to this principle is not "according to love." True Christians live according to love, extending the love of God to their neighbors. This means that the ethic of love accomplishes God's ultimate will for all humanity as Christians "conduct their lives according to love" (Rom. 14:15, my translation). As Paul says, "he that loves his neighbor has fulfilled the law" (Rom. 13:8).

It is because the future of the faithful is accomplished by God's love that Paul is absolutely certain of the ultimate triumph of God's justice. No power whatsoever is capable of interfering with the saving activity of love. Trying to imagine possible interfering forces, Paul distinguishes two groups. In the first he considers circumstances of daily life: tribulation, anguish, persecution, famine, nakedness, dangers, swords. He easily dismisses these obstacles to love's purpose as no actual contenders. In the second group Paul considers challenges that come from powers that operate outside of the earthly realm and are therefore beyond human control or will. With them he assumes an overpowering, defiant attitude. He declares: "neither death, nor life, nor angels, nor principalities, nor potentates, nor things present, nor things to come, not height, nor depth, nor anything else in all creation, will be able to separate us from the love of God" (Rom. 8:35 – 39). The triumph of love is secure.

God's gift of love should be received with expressions of thanksgiving because, as Paul's Gospel says, pouring his love to humanity and making a new creation in Christ, God did not absorb humanity but reconciled it to himself (2 Cor. 5; 17, 19). The new creation brought about by love, under whose control Christians live (2 Cor. 5:14), is not an amorphous conglomerate of passive robots who do God's will *en masse*. The Christian life of the new creation is not the boring life of an idealized perfection on this earth. It is the exciting life of taking seriously the life that is now lived in the midst of unpredictability and disorder. It is the life lived by the power of God's love that brings about faith and hope and issues in more love.

When life in bodies of flesh gives way to life in spirit bodies, faith and hope will have been replaced by sight. Now, looking through a glass darkly (1 Cor. 13:12), humans need to exercise faith and hope in God's love. But when life in the presence of God is achieved, love will continue to be the force behind all life. That is why Paul understood that among faith, hope and love, love is the greatest of the three, and affirmed that "love never ends" (1 Cor. 13:8).

III THE HOLY SPIRIT THAT HAS BEEN GIVEN TO US

The Gospel of Paul is the Gospel of the power of the Holy Spirit. This power has been in operation since Creation and will continue to be in operation through eternity. On two occasions in human history it acted most powerfully and most significantly, and it is still very active in a third. The first of these occasions was when it moved over the primeval waters setting the stage for God's first act on creation week. In 2 Corinthians 4:6 Paul makes this the foundation and model for the second occasion: "For it is the God who said, 'Let light shine out of darkness,' who has shone in our hearts to give the light of the knowledge of the glory of God in the face of Christ." Here the light shining out of darkness invokes Creation, and the glory of God in the face of Christ refers to the Resurrection. This demonstration of the power of the Spirit established a New Creation in which Christ is the Last Adam, the first of those who live by the power of the Spirit.

Since then, the dispensation of the Spirit has been in place and the Holy Spirit has been shining in the hearts of human beings, thus giving them the light that enables them "to know" about the resurrection. This dispensation is the third great accomplishment of the Holy Spirit. Since the beginning the Spirit has been making the divine light to shine in the darkness both by bringing about new cosmic realities and by enlightening human minds to appreciate those cosmic realities.

For Paul, the crucial thing is that Christians have been given the Spirit. Their life is now taking place on a different ecological system, even while they still live in the Fallen Creation of the first Adam. To live in the realm of Adam's creation is to live "in the flesh." In itself the flesh is not sinful. But the flesh is weak and, therefore, universally falls under the power of sin. Christians living in the flesh are not immune to falling under the power of sin; but they have also been given the Spirit (Rom. 5:5; 1 Th. 4:8). Thus, besides living in the flesh, they also live "in the Spirit." They are the beneficiaries of "the dispensation of the Spirit" (2 Cor. 3:8), living in a different ecology. An ecological system is what makes life possible as it is. The dispensation of the Spirit makes possible life in the Spirit. According to Paul, this is the *sine qua none* of being a Christian. Living in the Spirit, "the spiritual man judges all things, but is himself to be judged by no one" (1 Cor. 2:15). Christians, of course, will be judged by God, but they are privileged souls even while living in the flesh because the flesh is no longer the ecological system in which they live.

Paul takes for granted that all his converts have received the Spirit. For example, he does not ask the Galatians whether they have received the Spirit. Rather, he asks them on what basis did they receive the Spirit. That they received it is a given, and Paul expects them to know why they received it (Gal. 3:2). Warning the Thessalonians of the evils of adultery, especially when it is done wronging "a brother," Paul reminds them that Christians are not called to uncleanness, but to holiness. He justifies his admonition making the point that "whoever disregards this, disregards not man [Paul] but God, who gives the Holy Spirit to you" (1 Th. 4:8). That they have been receiving the Spirit is taken for granted. There is no such thing as a Christian who has not received the Spirit.

Because they have received the Spirit, Christians are expected to live by a higher moral compass. To the Romans Paul says "you are not in the flesh, you are in the Spirit, if the Spirit of God really dwells in you" (Rom. 8:9). With the Spirit dwelling in the individual, the Spirit is the one leading, and "all who are led by the Spirit of God are sons of God" (Rom. 8:14). Conversely, Paul says that "Any one who does not have the Spirit of Christ does not belong to him"

(Rom. 8:9). He makes the same point from the other side: "No one can say 'Jesus is Lord' except by the Holy Spirit" (1 Cor. 12:3). From these observations it is clear that those who have received the Spirit and dwell in the Spirit do not possess the Spirit. Rather they are possessed by the Spirit, and they are led by it; they belong to God and to Christ. To claim to have possession of the Spirit and to be able to order the Spirit to do this or that is not something Paul would have understood. Christians, as Paul repeatedly says, receive the Spirit and dwell in the Spirit only to be empowered and led by the Spirit. If that is not the case, they are not actually Christians.

Paul is very emphatic about the link that exists between what we earlier described as the second and the third manifestations of the power of the Spirit. He writes, "If the Spirit of him who raised Jesus from the dead dwells in you, he who raised Christ Jesus from the dead will give life to your mortal bodies also through his Spirit which dwells in you" (Rom. 8:11). Here Paul makes an explicit connection between the resurrection of Christ and the life of the believer who experiences the power of the Risen Christ while still living in the flesh, in a mortal body. To be a Christian is to live participating in the death and the resurrection of Christ. Thinking about the role of the Spirit, Paul's focus is on the power that brought about the resurrection of Christ and now empowers those who, on account of their identification with Christ, are sons of God.

In *To the Romans* and in *To the Galatians* Paul says that those who are led by the Spirit are not in bondage (Rom. 8:15); they are no longer "under the law" (Gal. 5:18). Christians, who have received the Spirit and dwell in it, belong to Christ. They live in the dispensation of the Spirit. They are led by the Spirit who is their Lord, and are, therefore, no longer under the Law. While life under the law is a form of bondage, life in Christ is in freedom. The Lord leads those who dwell in Him in freedom (2 Cor. 3:17). Life in the dispensation of the Spirit is characterized by freedom and peace (Rom. 8:6).

Paul does not make technical distinctions among the Spirit of God, the Spirit of Christ and the Holy Spirit. He use these terms interchangeably (Rom. 8:9; 14:17). What is accomplished in Christians through Christ for the benefit of humanity is done by God (2 Cor. 5:5; Gal . 4:7), who does everything by means of "one and the same Spirit" (1 Cor. 12:8 – 11; Rom. 8:11). For Paul, it is important to emphasize the singleness of the Spirit in the divine activity.

Paul is quite aware of the existence of many spirits who exercise their influence on human beings. The world in which he lived was full of supernatural spirits who brought both good and bad things to men and women. He makes clear that God's action in and through the Spirit was not being accomplished by various and sundry intermediaries, each one in charge of a particular task. All the tasks and ministrations carried out by God are the work of one and the same Spirit, no matter how Paul designates him in his writings.

Besides the divine Spirit, Paul understands that each human being is constituted with a spirit. Each person is a unit which functions integrally as such. He tells the Thessalonians, "May the God of peace himself sanctify you wholly, and may your spirit and soul and body be kept sound and blameless" (1 Th. 5:23). The second part of this sentence is epexegetical; it elaborates on the meaning of the first. To be kept sound and blameless is to be sanctified. The spirit, the soul and the body are not parts of the whole, but ways of conceiving the whole. Each person is a spirit when seen as an active force, a soul when looked at as a living thing, and a body when seen as a physical presence. None of the three is ever separated from the other two. Paul refers to himself as a spirit. He writes, "For God is my witness, whom I worship in my spirit, in the gospel of his Son" (Rom. 1:9, my translation). He also says that when Christians pray "it is the Spirit himself bearing witness with our spirit that we are children of God" (Rom. 8:16). He asks the Philippians to be united as they faced opposition to their "faith of the gospel" and also to conduct themselves in a manner "worthy of the gospel." To this end, Paul tells them to "stand firm in one spirit and one mind" [in the Greek original "one spirit and one soul"] (Phil. 1:27). In these cases Paul is using the words spirit and soul to refer to the whole person, not a part of it.

The mind, on the other hand, is a faculty of the person. Paul advises Christians to set the mind on the Spirit, rather than to set the mind on the flesh. He writes, "To set the mind on the flesh is death, but to set the mind on the Spirit is life and peace" (Rom. 8:6). In other words, living in this present age, Christians can choose to live in the Fallen Creation, the ecological system under the power of sin and death, or to live in the New Creation, that is under the power of the Spirit that raised Christ from the dead. Two different powers are now in operation. One is the power of "the god of this world," that is Satan, who is effective through the power of sin that brings about death. The other is the power of the Spirit that raised Christ from death and is effective as the power of the Gospel that brings about life.

Writing to those who apparently have not understood the significance of the gospel of Christ, Paul says, "For the law of the Spirit of life in Christ Jesus has set me free from the law of sin and death" (Rom. 8:2). In this way those who are led by the Spirit enjoy peace and live free from the power of sin. They live in a different ecology. They breathe the atmosphere of the Spirit which transforms them from one degree of glory to another by the power of the Risen Christ (2 Cor. 3:18). This does not mean that they have ceased being mortal bodies of flesh. It means that they have ceased being servants of the spiritual forces of evil that have become dominant within the Fallen Creation.

"The Last Adam became a life-giving Spirit" (1 Cor. 15:45). The first being of the New Creation did not just receive life after having been dead in a tomb. The Christian Gospel is not merely a story about a crucified dead man who now lives because God raised him from the dead. The Gospel of Paul proclaims a New Creation by the Spirit who gives life. The Risen Christ is the one in whom all those who believe live within the New Creation by the power of the Spirit that raised Christ from the dead. Christianity is the religion of the New Creation in which human beings may now experience life in the Spirit, and "worship God in the Spirit, glory in Christ Jesus, and put no confidence in the flesh" (Phil. 3:3).

In Paul thinking, Christians who have the Spirit are sealed by the Spirit for a future that is different from the one to which those who live under the power of sin and death are destined. This sealing is described by Paul as a guarantee, a down payment (an *arrabon*) that ensures the full payment of what has been promised (2 Cor. 1:22; 5:5). The freedom and peace enjoyed by those who live in the Spirit and are guided by the Spirit is a foretaste in this "present evil age" (Gal 1:4) of life as full spiritual beings with spiritual bodies (1 Cor. 15:44) — that is, life in the resurrection body of the Age to Come.

Those who in this life experience changes from glory to glory, "being renewed every day" as they are "worked over" by the Spirit to receive "an eternal weight of glory beyond all comparison," are the tangible demonstration that the purpose for which humankind had been created by God in the first place is being fulfilled (2 Cor. 4:17; 5:5). Thus the final manifestation of the justice of God, carried on by the Spirit that transforms and energizes human spirits in the likeness of the Risen Christ, will have been accomplished. Living in Christ by the power of the Spirit Christians "become the righteousness of God" effectively at work (2 Cor. 5:21).

IV We Are Children of Promise

One of the most telling things to be taken into account when trying to understand anyone's theology is the metaphor at its center. All theological language is analogical or metaphorical. There is no other way for us to talk about God. As humans we are limited by our concepts and symbols. We can only speak of God and of God's affairs using our concepts, our language with its semantic limitations.

We may speak of God as our father, but no one is to understand that literally. It only makes sense metaphorically. It is most instructive to note how the authors of the Old Testament avoided this way of describing God. Since they were in a constant struggle to make clear that Yahve was not to be confused with the fertility gods of the cults that were popular in Canaan, they refrained from speaking of Yahve as a father and never used the feminine form of the word "god." When speaking about a female goddess of their neighbors, they referred to her with the masculine plural "gods." For them the metaphor "father" was not useful on account of its cultural connotations to fertility.

Most stories of creation from the ancient Near East describe battles and say that the body of the defeated divinity was used as the material with which the world was made. Thus the earth is of divine origin. One of the most theologically significant breakthroughs in the Old Testament is to say that "by the word of the Lord the heavens were made, and all their host by the breath of his mouth" (Ps. 33:6). This places God at a distance from his creation, breaking any physical connection. The story in Genesis 1 is an elaboration of this insight. Its significance is that it links God and his creation by a "word." For the ancient Hebrews words were very concrete, but were not material.

The Old Testament's main concern is to affirm God's activity in history, and central to the historical experience of Israel is the making of a covenant between God and Abraham which was later redefined at Sinai by the giving of the law through Moses. Thus the covenant metaphor became central to Hebrew theology. The prophets and the psalmists never cease to remind the people that their most important duty is to have "loyalty to the covenant." Unfortunately the Hebrew word for this phrase, *chesed,* is most commonly translated as mercy, or loving kindness. Such mistranslation obscures that the word refers to the need for those who are bound by a covenant to keep the terms to which they have agreed. Quite often the prophets diagnose the troubles the people are experiencing as due to their lack of *chesed*; by contrast, Yahve's is rock-solid. The *chesed* of the people is like the morning dew that evaporates as soon as the day warms up. Deuteronomy is a long plea for the people to remain loyal to the covenant. Their wellbeing in the land will depend on their obedience to the covenant stipulations. Deuteronomic theology became the basic orthodoxy of Post-exilic Judaism. Thus, the notion that the people and God are bound together by a covenant became central to Judaism and Christianity.

It became natural, therefore, for most students of the Bible to read the whole Bible with the covenant as the central metaphor that establishes the relationship between God and the people. This means that Christianity is understood in terms of a covenant in which the law given at Sinai still plays a central role. Only those who are obedient to the commandments can claim to be part of the people with whom God made a covenant. It is understandable that some of the first Christians understood that Christianity was another form of Judaism, just like the Pharisees, the Sadducees, the Essenes, the Nazarenes, etc. This meant that Christians still went to the Jerusalem temple to worship, especially at the annual feasts, and keeping of the law was their identity badge.

There were, however, some Christians who from the beginning saw some tension between an identity centered on the law and an identity centered on Christ. Both the gospel *According to Matthew* and the gospel *According to John* have Jesus issuing new commandments as a way to solve this problem. Paul, on the other hand, was more radical in this respect. He totally distinguished Christianity from the covenant made at Sinai. He found another Old Testament metaphor to be central to the relationship between God and His people.

Paul's theology is based on two texts of Scripture. One is the answer which was given to Habakkuk when he questioned the justice of God after seeing what was taking place in Israel. Habakkuk reports that he set himself on a tower to see what the Lord would have to say concerning his complaint (Hab. 2:1). The Lord answered Habakkuk telling him that what he is about to hear might not be satisfactory at first, but time would prove that "it will not lie." The core of God's answer to Habakkuk is that those who are not upright will fail, "but the righteous shall live by his faith" (Hab. 2:4). In other words, the righteous may not see the justice of God in action, but still they must live trusting God. Faith is the essential ingredient in a good life.

The other key text for Paul is the report of the encounter of Abraham with God, at which time God promised Abraham three things. In the first place, the land in which he wanders as a foreigner will be his. Secondly, his descendants will be as numerous as the stars of the heavens and the sand of the sea. Finally, through his descendants all the nations of the earth will be blessed. As time went on, Abraham complained to Yahve that he was still childless and a slave born in his house would become his heir. To this the Lord answered by taking Abraham outside the tent and saying: "'Look toward heaven, and number the stars, if you are able to number them . . . . So shall your descendants be. And he believed the Lord; and he reckoned it to him as righteousness" (Gen. 15:6).

What God gave Abraham was a threefold promise, and Abraham did the right thing when he believed God.

Indeed, the only way to take hold of a promise is to believe the one who makes it. If those to whom a promise has been made do not believe the one making the promise, they heard some words but do not have a promise. Faith is the only thing that can appropriate a promise. Why did God reckon Abraham righteous? Because by taking God at his word, he did exactly what he needed to do. An action is righteous when it is what God expects.

These two texts of Scripture complement each other. They tie righteousness to faith in a promise. For Paul, at the heart of the human-divine relationship is a promise. Rather than to understand the word that relates God to his creatures as a law, Paul understands it as a promise. A promise is totally different from a covenant because a covenant requires specific actions from those signing it, and can be broken by either one of them. A promise, on the other hand, requires that the one receiving it believes the one making it, and its fulfillment depends only on the one making it. When God told Abraham that the land of his sojourns would be his, his descendants would be uncountable, and they would be the agents for the blessing of all nations, nothing had pressured God to make these promises to Abraham, and nothing was expected from Abraham. These promises demonstrated God's grace, and they became effective by Abraham's faith. Here Paul found the basis for understanding how the apocalyptic death and resurrection of Christ fitted into the human-divine ongoing relationship.

For Paul, Abraham is not just the father of Isaac and Jacob and the twelve tribes of Israel. His descendants are not just the Israelites who received the law at Sinai. The land that was promised was not just the land of Canaan. According to Paul, God promised Abraham that his descendants would inherit "the world." The promise was not part of the giving of the law at Sinai, but came "through the righteousness of faith" (Rom. 4:13). The "heirs" of Abraham are not just the "adherents of the law." If that were the case "faith is null and the promise is void" (Rom. 4:14). Of course, even to imagine that is, for Paul, totally ridiculous. He then states why the promise cannot come from the law. Rather than to provide the promise, "the law brings wrath, but where there is no law there is no transgression" (Rom. 4:15). If at the core of the human-divine relationship is the law, and the function of the law is to define transgressions, then the wrath of God which punishes transgressions is the unavoidable result. In other words, the law takes humans down the path to a dead end.

Having established that, Paul brings out the alternative. "That is why it depends on faith, in order that the promise may rest on grace and be guaranteed to all his descendants — not only to the adherents of the law but also to those who share the faith of Abraham, for he is the father of us all" (Rom. 4:16). Yes, Abraham is the father of the Israelites who received the law at Sinai. More significant, however, is that Abraham believed the one who promised him heirs. So now Paul expands on the strength of Abraham's faith. Given the fact that he was one hundred years old and Sarah was well past menopause, their physical condition made it look impossible for God to fulfill his promise. Paul admires the fact that Abraham's faith did not weaken in the least on account of Sarah's and his own lack of fertility. "In hope he believed against hope, that he should become the father of many nations, as he had been told. . . . No distrust made him waver concerning the promise of God, but he grew strong in his faith as he gave glory to God" (Rom. 4:18, 20). Considering the faith of Abraham, Paul makes clear what was that Abraham believed, and refers to an important philosophical notion.

Abraham received the promise of descendants "in the presence of the God in whom he believed, who gives life to the dead and names the things that are not as well as the things that are" (Rom. 4:17, my translation). Abraham did not believe the promise. He believed the God who made him the promise. Which God was the one promising? The promise was made by the God who gives life to the dead — an obvious reference to the raising of Christ and the giving of eschatological life to those dead in the transgressions that spark the wrath of God.

With these words Paul presents a God who stands over creation in a most particular way. The God in whom Abraham placed his faith is not only the God who created all that is. He also "names" the things that are not. His God bridges the gap between the things that are determined in space and time and the things that are pure ideas in God. He controls the frontier between potentiality and actuality. That is the realm of pure freedom, the realm of the Spirit that moved over the waters before creation, raised Christ from the dead and gives life to believers. This is the realm of miracles.

Paul bases Abraham's faith on his understanding that the God who made him the promise, whose promise he believed, is the God who created what is and controls what has no existence. Non-existence is a very abstract notion, but Paul is an educated man of the Hellenistic Age. By describing creation in this way he highlights the power of God to do what is apparently impossible. Abraham's God would have no difficulty fulfilling his promise to give descendants to two old people who were already infertile. Knowing the God he believed in, Abraham was "fully convinced that God was able to do what he had promised" (Rom. 4:21). For Paul, full conviction is essential to faith.

The one who demonstrated such faith is the father of us all. His descendants are not just those who descend from the Israelites who entered into a covenant centered on the law. He is the father of those from any nation who exercise faith. Thus the promise that all nations would be blessed through Abraham is being fulfilled as Paul writes to Jews and Gentiles in Rome. As Paul sees it, "Christ became a servant to the circumcision on account of God's truthfulness to the promises made to the patriarchs so that the Gentiles might glorify God on account of his mercy" (Rom. 15:8 – 9, my translation). Giving the promise to Abraham, God already had in mind how His blessings would benefit both the circumcised and the uncircumcised.

Quite often Paul found himself having to defend his ministry because other Christian apostles disseminated attacks against him and his understanding of the Gospel. Doing this with the Christians at Corinth he reminds them that when he was among them with his colleagues they did not engage in double talk. They only spoke in positive, confirming affirmations of God's activity. He insists to them that in Christ it is always a YES. "That is why we utter the Amen through him." Defending himself he declares, "it is God who establishes us with you in Christ." Then he links the ministry of Silvanus, Timothy and himself to the Gospel they are preaching with the explanation, "For all the promises of God find their YES in him [Christ]" (2 Cor. 1:18 – 21). This same linkage is found at the introduction of his letter *To the Romans,* "Paul, a servant of Jesus Christ, called to be an apostle, set apart for the gospel of God, which he promised before hand through his prophets in the holy scriptures" (Rom. 1:1). The promise to Abraham has found its confirmation in the Gospel to which he has been called to be an apostle.

Paul establishes his identity in his being a child of Abraham, not in the flesh but in the promise (Rom 9:8). By basing his theology on the metaphor that the link between God and humanity is a promise, Paul effectively disallows any nationalistic understanding of salvation. Jews and Gentiles stand on the same footing when the model to be imitated is the faith of Abraham, rather than the circumcision of Isaac. In Paul's theology, Christian identity cannot be based on the law. It can only be based on Christ, the One who fulfills the promise of God. On that account, repeatedly Paul relativizes circumcision as an identity marker (Rom. 2:25; 1 Cor. 7:19; Gal. 5:6; 6:15). This became the flash point in the confrontations between Paul and the apostles who preached a Christianity that was another form of Judaism. To them the covenant was still the basic metaphor for understanding the human divine relationship. Of course, circumcision was the objective marker at the frontier between the people of God and those outside. God had made a covenant only with the Jews. To Paul, Christianity was the fulfillment of the promise that through Abraham all nations would be blessed. The Gospel of the promise eliminated all the markers set at the frontiers that separate human beings from each other. As the fulfilment and the reaffirmation of the promise, Christ is available to all without distinctions. Those who like Abraham are fully convinced of God's ability to keep a promise, even when a reality check would make it look impossible, are the children of God by the power of the Gospel that fulfills God's promise.

V
Keep Your Hearts and Your Minds

As an apostle of the Gospel of God's righteousness demonstrated in the cross and the resurrection of Christ, Paul's main concern is that his listeners participate in the life of the Risen Christ and change their manner of living. For this to happen, however, they must understand his gospel and its implications for the conduct of daily life in this world. He, therefore, insists that Christians must exercise their mental power to the fullest. While also appealing to their feelings and emotions, which he does quite effectively in his letters *To the Corinthians I* and *II, To the Thessalonians I, To the Philippians* and *To Philemon*, and he shows real impatience and anger in his letter *To the Galatians*, he does not play with emotions and feelings like a demagogue. Nor does he make a melodrama of the Christ event. His prevailing appeal is to the rational powers of his audience.

Reason may be viewed both as that which gives the mind the structure within which any thought is possible and as the steps taken by the mind according to rules agreed-upon on the basis of common reason. Following these rules one may argue for the superiority of one proposition over another. Conclusions arrived at without following these rules are judged unreasonable or illogical. A person who lacks the built-in structures of reason is said to have lost his or her mind, be retarded, or mentally ill. Arguments which do not stand the test of logic are said to be weak or flawed.

It is frustrating to hear a speaker going from here to there without any intelligent connections. At the end we wonder what it was all about. Maybe we were entertained and we feel good about it, but we don't take any lasting thing home with us. On the other hand, it is a delight to read or listen to an argument that is well articulated. Even if at the end we find it unconvincing we admire the reasoning deployed in its presentation. Paul's letters amply display his skills to reason with his readers. We may disagree with Paul's premises, but we learn a great deal about his faith by the way he expounds and defends it.

Paul trusts the ability of his audience to use their minds and reason properly. He writes, "I speak as to sensible [thinking] men; judge for yourselves what I say" (1 Cor. 10:15). After having had a serious disagreement with the Corinthians, he writes to them, "Examine yourselves, to see whether you are holding to your faith. Test yourselves. Do you not realize that Jesus Christ is in you? — unless indeed you fail to meet the test! I hope you will find out that we have not failed [to meet the test to which faith is to be put]" (2 Cor. 13:5 – 6). Paul does not wish to have others evaluate the Corinthians as to their faith. Neither is he going to do it himself. He trusts the ability of all those who live in Christ to test themselves. He also expects them to evaluate the reasonableness of what he tells them. Their judgment is valid.

Paul loses his patience with the Galatians who overlook the evidence of their own experience, against which there can be no argument, and, rather harshly, calls them "foolish" (Gal. 3:1, the Greek reads *morons*). To the Corinthians, who consider themselves strong people who "know all" (2 Cor. 8:12), "own everything" (2 Cor. 3:21) and affirm that "all things are lawful" (1 Cor. 6:12), Paul says, "Brethren, do not be children in your thinking, be babes in evil, but in thinking be mature" (1 Cor. 14:20). He further pleads with them, "Come to your right mind" (1 Cor. 15:34).

Describing the wrath of God at work in the pagans who have been delivered by God to their sinful ways, he locates their problem in their mind. According to Paul, the power and the glory of God in evidence within creation are within the mind's reach (Rom. 1:20). Failing to recognize them is due to the senseless heart of those who change the truth for a lie. Their hearts have been darkened and their reasoning has become futile (Rom. 1:21). When the heart, the seat of being where desires, plans and purposes are harbored, is in the dark, the mind fails to perform dutifully. Those in this condition are held responsible for their futile ways.

Paul also recognizes that there are Gentiles who live righteous lives and argues that knowledge of the law is no guarantee of righteousness. It is not the hearers of the law, but the doers of the law who are righteous before God. It happens, therefore, that "when Gentiles who do not have the law do by nature what the law requires . . . They show that what the law requires [Greek = "the works of the law"] is written on their hearts" (Rom. 2:14, 15). On the other hand, there are Gentiles who have darkened "senseless minds" and fail to see what is, according to Paul, quite visible in creation (Rom. 1:20 – 21). To be noticed in this connection is that Paul connects the law written in the hearts of some Gentiles and the conscience that "bears witness" together with the law in those hearts. In this Paul agrees with the Greek philosophers who thought that the conscience could only accuse the person who has done something wrong. Paul gives the same negative role to the law. Moreover, he recognizes that the law and the conscience are exposed to rationalizations that "accuse and excuse" (Rom. 2:14 – 15). These observations on Paul's part reveal a perceptive understanding of the interior life where decisions are made and characters are formed.

Paul's advice to Christians is: "Do not allow this age to mold you according to its designs. Rather, be metamorphosed with a new mind from above so that you may evaluate what is the will of God, what is good and acceptable and perfect" (Rom. 12:2, my translation). A mind renewed from above by the Holy Spirit is here given extraordinary power, and Paul thinks every Christian should be in possession of such a mind. Each Christian is an arbiter of the will of God. Paul is not one who pretends to dictate God's will. He recognizes that each Christian has the ability to discern God's will by the use of the mind, thus making everyone personally accountable.

Paul does not privilege the mind as such, however. He very carefully qualifies the effective moral agent as the mind renewed from above. He does not envision his churches as communities of knowledgeable insiders, but as communities in which all members are guided by the Spirit and have the freedom to be willing servants of God. Authority belongs to the human mind enlightened by the Spirit that raised Christ from the dead. Such a mind seeks the good of the neighbor. Paul does not pass out rules to be followed according to his own criteria. The sequence in the advice he gives to the Thessalonians is most revealing in this regard. He tells them, "Test [consider, evaluate] everything; hold fast what is good, abstain from every form of evil" (1 Th. 5:21 – 22). Paul grants them the responsibility to evaluate things and to determine by themselves what is good and what is evil. He trusts the power of their minds. The mind renewed by the Spirit is not a prudish, or libertine, or split, or closed mind. A tidy mind has been arranged by an ideology and takes a defensive posture against all others because it fears becoming disarrayed by external interactions. The renewed mind is a simple, reasonable mind that is free from internal conflicts and open to investigate the realities of life. It causes the heart to be humble and at peace. The Spirit gives the mind integrity and freedom.

When Paul sends Onesimus back to Philemon, confident that Philemon will accept as a brother in Christ the runaway slave who is now Paul's son in the faith, he does not appeal to his apostolic authority and command Philemon to do as he is told. He is confident that Philemon knows how to treat Onesimus and that he will do even more than what Paul might suggest. Explicitly, Paul does not tell Philemon to acquiesce to his demands, but to be free to exercise his own determinations (Philem. *passim*). This attitude of Paul is also evident in the advice he gives the Corinthians about what to do at their assemblies: "Let two or three prophets speak, and let the others weigh what is said" (1 Cor. 14:29). Paul does not think everything said by prophets is to be taken on authority. It must be thought over, evaluated, judged by the enlightened mind of the listeners.

Paul respects the ability of his audiences to use their minds effectively, especially since as Christians they have been given the Spirit and enjoy the renewed mind that is not like the futile mind of those who fail to see the truth of God's power and divinity in creation. Advising the Romans how to live while waiting for "the redemption of our bodies," Paul reminds them of the help provided by the Spirit. Among other things, he tells them that "the Spirit himself intercedes for us with sighs too deep for words," thus making their prayers effective. Then God, who "searches the hearts of men and knows the spiritual mind," recognizes such prayers because "the Spirit intercedes for the saints according to the will of God" (Rom. 8:23 – 27). The communication of believers with their God is through the active involvement of the spiritual mind and the heart. It is where the leading and the intercession of the Spirit takes place.

Paul starts his letter to the Philippians voicing his prayer for them. "It is my prayer that your love may abound more and more, with knowledge and all discernment, so that you may approve what is excellent" (Phil. 1:9 – 10). His first wish for all Christians is that they develop the tools with which to determine what is excellent. In this context he then urges them to share the mind of their Lord. He tells them, "complete my joy by being of the same mind, having the same love, being in full accord and of one mind . . . . Have this mind among yourselves, which you have in Christ Jesus" (Phil. 2:2, 5). The Greek original is somewhat vague. Another possible reading is, "This thinking be in you, which was also in Christ Jesus." This thinking is the advice he has just given them: "Do nothing from selfishness or conceit, but in humility count others better than yourselves. Let each of you look not only to his own interests, but also to the interests of others" (Phil. 2:3 – 4). This was the thinking of Christ Jesus when, as pointed out in the following verse, though being in the form of god he emptied himself and took the form of a servant. To bring the letter to a conclusion, Paul writes: "Finally, brethren, whatever is true, whatever is honorable, whatever is just, whatever is pure, whatever is lovely, whatever is gracious, if there is any excellence, if there is anything worthy of praise, think about these things" (Phil. 4:8). Paul is concerned about the way in which the mind is used, but does not set up rules. He only offers broad guidelines.

Paul also gives ample evidence of his own ability to build arguments using the tools of logic which he, a well-educated Hellenistic Pharisee, evidently possessed. As noted in a previous meditation, he constructs a wonderful *midrash* on the story of Moses' descent from Mt. Sinai with a shining face (2 Cor. 3:4 – 18), as well as of Jeremiah's visit to the potter's workshop (Rom. 9:21 – 23). He does a good job allegorizing the story of the two sons of Abraham and their mothers (Gal. 4:21 – 31). Occasionally, Paul limits the meaning of a word by bringing two passages from Scripture together in which the word is used (see Rom 9:33 for "stone") On other occasions, Paul quotes a Scriptural text and elaborates on a linguistic detail (see 1 Cor. 15:27; Gal. 3:16). These are typical rabbinic ways of arguing.

In Galatians, Paul builds an argument *ad hominem*, an appeal to common sense. If no one expects another human being to add clauses unilaterally to a contract which has already been signed, is it logical to think that God did such a thing? (Gal. 3:15). In Romans he builds a more complicated argument *de minori ad maiorem*, from the lesser to the greater. If it is granted that "this" is the case, how much more should "that" be the case, because everyone agrees that "that" stands logically higher than "this." (Rom. 5:10, 15, 17; 11:12, 24).

One of the most telling evidences of Paul's respect for the reasoning powers of his audience is a prominent feature of his writing style. He is a consummate practitioner of the rhetorical question, which is a most effective way to invite readers to give some thought to what is being said. Rhetorical questions engage the mind of the listener and tacitly invite participation in a dialogue, even while not demanding an answer. It is most revealing to count such questions in Paul's letters: there are 17 in *To the Galatians*, 18 in *To the Corinthians II*, 47 in *To the Romans*, 81 in *To the Corinthians I*. In the letters where he discusses important theological questions as he argues against the views of others, Paul uses them extensively. No doubt there are fewer in *To the Galatians* because it is shorter.

Some rhetorical questions exhibit the dead end of an argument, for example: "Shall we say that the law is sin?" (Rom. 7:7); "Is God the God of Jews only?" (Rom. 3:29); "Did the word of God originate with you, or are you the only ones it has reached?" (1 Cor. 14:36). Some ridicule what Paul's opponents claim to be his view, for example; "Are we to continue in sin that grace may abound?" (Rom. 6:1); "Is Christ, then an agent of sin?" (Gal. 2:17); "Do we not have the right to be accompanied by a wife?" (1 Cor. 9:5). Some call attention to what is obvious, for example: "Do you not have homes to eat and drink in?" (1 Cor. 11:22); "If God is for us, who is against us?" (Rom. 8:31). Some serve to introduce analogies, for example, "If lifeless instruments . . . do not give distinct notes, how will anyone know what is played? If the bugle gives an indistinct sound, who will get ready for battle?" (1 Cor. 14:7 – 8). Some call to mind experience, for example; "If . . .all speak in tongues, and outsiders or unbelievers enter, will they not say that you are mad?" (1 Cor. 14:23); "Did you receive the Spirit by works of law, or by hearing of faith?" (Gal. 3:2); "What has become of the satisfaction you felt?" (Gal. 4:15). Some anticipate objections or slanders, for example: "But some will ask, 'How are the dead raised? With what kind of body do they come?" (1 Cor. 15:35); "Why not do evil that good may come? — as some people slanderously charge us with saying." (Rom. 3:8); "You will say to me then, 'Why does he still find fault?'" (Rom. 9:19). All his rhetorical questions reveal an agile mind at work by one who trusts the agile minds in his audience.

Paul's letters are not Socratic dialogues. Its readers must imaginatively provide what Paul's conversation partners have said. As reported by Plato, Socrates consistently limits himself to asking questions. His conversation partners provide the answers. Socrates then explores the implications, or the basis of the answer by asking a question about the answer. Like Socrates, Paul is quite conscious of his limits, and trusts unconditionally the reasoning powers of his audience. By means of questions, he guides his readers in the exploration of the issue at hand.

Repeatedly Paul refuses to judge others, expecting that they are quite capable of deciding by themselves, as their decisions will eventually be judged by God (Rom. 2:16). Since Christians are servants of Christ, only their Master has the authority to judge their performance. No Christian has been given the authority to judge a fellow servant (Rom. 14:4). At Rome some were despising others who did not eat meat, and these were condemning those who ate it. Paul considers these actions contrary to the Gospel. There were also those who separated a day of the week as special and others who considered all days equally special since they were now living in the New Creation. Again, on account of these differences, members of the Christian community were despising and condemning each other. Paul's answer to the situation is a revelation of the value he placed on the ability of Christians to serve their Lord according to the dictates of their minds. Advising the Romans who have different opinions about Sabbaths and foods, Paul writes, "Let everyone be fully convinced in his own mind" (Rom. 14:5) as to what he/she should do, and not despise or condemn a fellow servant who is convinced that he/she should do otherwise. Paul sums up his analysis of the situation with a beatitude: "Happy is he who has no reason to judge himself for what he approves" (Rom. 14:22). If your conscience judges you for what you approve, you lack full conviction. Full conviction in partnership with the Spirit is a blessed state of being (1 Th. 1:5). It is the determining factor. When such is the case, Christians live in full assurance. To be noticed is that, while Paul reminds the Romans that all must appear before the judgment seat of God (Rom. 14:10), he considers that individual Christians have been empowered to judge themselves according to his definition of sin (Rom. 14:23).

According to Paul, the renewed, critical mind must be actively involved in all aspects of life, most significantly in worship. Considering the Corinthians' predilection for the gift of speaking in tongues, Paul insists that when Christians come together to worship they should be one body, not a group of individuals. They should "strive to excel in building up the church" (1 Cor. 14:12), and do everything "decently and in order" (1 Cor. 14:40). Within this framework, he reflects on the speaking in tongues at such a gathering. His first instruction is that the one speaking in tongues "should pray for the power to interpret." He then explains why this is necessary. "For if I pray in a tongue, my spirit prays but my mind is unfruitful. What am I to do? I will pray with the spirit and I will pray with the mind also; I will sing with the spirit and will sing with the mind also" (1 Cor. 14:14 – 15). Praying and singing in tongues, for Paul, is not a way of building up the church because in such activity the mind is disengaged. When praying and singing with the mind, all those present can say "Amen" to the praying, the singing and the blessing because they have understood what is being said and done (1 Cor. 14:16). For life in community, the mind is indispensable.

As Paul sees it, The Spirit does not impose himself on the mind in a way that frustrates or annuls the work of the mind. The authorization of the mind by the Spirit does not render the person irrational. The Spirit does not veto the mind. It opens up the mind to explore the things of the Spirit (Rom. 8:6). In a well-integrated person, the Spirit and the mind do not work in contraposition. In healthy Christians faith and reason are not at odds with each other. Rather, the Christian way of being launches faith and reason on a joint enterprise.

There should not be any doubt as to the central role played by the mind in the theology of Paul. Evidently, Paul was an intellectual, precisely because he loved truth and wisdom, considered the right use of the mind as the instrument to be used for their attainment, and respected the ability of his fellow Christians to use their minds properly. He may have disdained "the wisdom of the world," but only because he considered Christ, the power and the wisdom of God infinitely superior (1 Cor. 1:24). Lamentably, the world failed to recognize its superiority.

It may be claimed that in one significant aspect Paul surpasses the ancient philosophers. Plato, probably the most prominent among them, may be considered the paradigm of worldly wisdom. Plato considers knowledge of the true, the good and the beautiful to be the ultimate achievement of a human mind. Only philosophers who follow the proper rules of logic and know how to deal with ideas are able to attain such knowledge on account of the power of reason. For a society to achieve goodness and justice, according to Plato, philosophers should be kings. He thought so because even though he recognizes that actions have more than one cause, following Socrates, Plato thought that knowledge had the power to bring about action in accord with it.

Like all ancient philosophers, from Socrates to Plotinus, Plato is concerned ultimately with how to live and die well. Philosophy, the pursuit of wisdom, had to do with the way to live. These philosophers teach that reason is the instrument for the attainment of wisdom and that, even if there may be other motivations involved, reason also provides the motivations for living the good life that reason prescribes.

Paul agrees with his philosophical contemporaries on the centrality of reason in order to consider options and evaluate them properly. Unlike ancient philosophers, however, he understands that only the power of the Holy Spirit, rather than that of reason, could motivate an individual to act according to what he/she thought to be the will of God. Paul realizes that the one who knows what is good and just is not naturally empowered by reason to do what is good and just. Paul confesses, "For I do not do the good I want, but the evil I do not want is what I do" (Rom. 7:19). For him, it is the power of the Holy Spirit in the heart that renews the mind and empowers individuals to live the good life. Paul discovered that humans need an exterior power to transfer what the mind approves to what the body does. In order to actually do the good and the beautiful, Paul recognizes the need of the love of God that pours the Spirit into human hearts.

Socrates and his followers understood that most people act on the basis of what things appear to be. It is necessary, therefore, to train the mind in order to penetrate into things past their outward appearance. In other words, it is necessary to attain knowledge of them. Once one has grasped the truth of things by going past their external appearance, reason itself causes one to act on the basis of the knowledge one has gained. To lead the good life, then, is to be constantly on guard against the deceptions of appearances.

Paul also understands that to live the good life it is necessary to be on guard, but not against the outward appearance of things. The struggle is not an intellectual struggle against appearances to be carried out aided by a trained mind. Paul understands that the struggle is a spiritual one carried out in the heart, the seat of being. Decisions are made in the realm where desires, experiences, instincts and purposes are in constant tension within people who live in a fallen creation, where the power of sin is strongly felt. Decisions are made in the heart. The heart is not primarily the seat of the emotions, but most significantly the agent of the will. It is a realm more integral to the personality than the realm of the mind where knowledge is gained and stored. Of course, it is very important for the mind to evaluate information and to arrive at proper conclusions. The person, however, makes decisions and initiates actions in what, following Hebraic terminology, Paul calls the heart. There is where the Spirit brings about convictions that cause people to act.

The Gospel is not just a matter for the mind, a message that must be understood. It is a way of being in the world that must be lived. The Gospel may reach the individual through the mind, and the mind has a task to do with it, considering its premises, judging its arguments, evaluating its goals. But the Gospel must find its home in the heart, the seat of being. It cannot get to the heart without passing through the mind, but it is not effective unless it settles in the heart, changing it in the process. As Paul puts it, the heart must be circumcised (Rom. 2:29). The power of sin in it must be expurgated. The Christian has a mind renewed from above and a circumcised heart. Paul's promise to his converts is that "the peace of God, which passes all understanding, will keep your hearts and your minds in Christ Jesus" (Phil. 4:7). To keep the mind and the heart together is to live by faith and reason. The love of God that the Spirit pours into the heart does not dislodge the unity of the mind and the heart. It strengthens it. In the Christian, faith and reason abide as one.

It is into the heart of sinners that the Holy Spirit pours the love of God that starts the process of salvation (Rom. 5:5). Faith is a matter of the heart. It is in the heart that the word of faith is stored (Rom 10:8). Paul then states, "For man believes with his heart, and so is justified" (Rom. 10:10). When a pagan enters a Christian service and hears someone prophesying, he finds "the secrets of his heart disclosed; and so, falling on his face, he will worship God" (1 Cor. 14:25). At the final judgment God "will bring to light the things now hidden in darkness and will disclose the purposes of the heart" (1 Cor. 4:5). Even now God "searches the heart of man" (Rom. 8:27); therefore, since God "tests our hearts" humans should not endeavor merely to please men but to please God (1 Th. 2:4).

From the texts we have reviewed, it is evident that the relationship of humans with God takes place in the heart. It is in the heart that the Holy Spirit dwells (Gal. 4:6; 2 Cor. 1:22). As noted, it is in the heart that one believes and the word of faith is kept, therefore, the obedience of faith is "obedience from the heart" (Rom. 6:17). It is also in the heart that a person makes ultimate decisions, arrives at full convictions, or is established and the will is activated. Therefore, God's evaluation of the person is centered in a search of the heart. But all the gifts of God can only reach the heart through the mind.

In *To the Corinthians I* Paul answers questions which the Corinthians have sent him in a letter (1 Cor. 7:1). One of the questions had to do with matters having to do with marriage. Answering, Paul discusses whether or not one should marry. He makes the point that those who decide to marry should go ahead. Even if time is short and the Lord is coming any day now, it is no sin to marry.

On the other hand, "whoever is firmly established in his heart, being under no necessity but having his desire under control, and has determined this in his heart, to keep her as his betrothed, he will do well" (1 Cor. 7:37). It is quite striking how Paul places this very difficult decision as something that is established in the heart, but the determination on which the decision was made took place in the mind. Reflecting a similar understanding of how a person is constituted and acts, the apostle's desire for the Thessalonians is, "may the Lord make you increase and abound in love to one another and to all men, as we do to you, so that he may establish your hearts unblamable in holiness before our God and Father" (1 Th. 3:12 – 13).

As the seat of being, the place where the Gospel which is a way of being finds itself lodged and exercises its power on the will of the believer, the heart plays a pivotal role in the salvation of men and women. It is the central core served by the mind where the ultimate decisions of life and death are made. For Paul the heart is not only the organ of emotions and feelings. It is the seat of being where faith is exercised, convictions arrived at by the mind are firmly established, and the mind renewed from above and set on the things of the Spirit has stamped its character. In a healthy, integrated person, there cannot be tension between the reasons of the mind and the faith of the heart.

VI GOD SENT FORTH HIS SON

Paul's Gospel is about what God has done, is doing, and will do to realize the purpose of His creation. In his account of God's activity, of course, Jesus performs the indispensable task that demonstrates God's justice at work. He is the one who subjects all the evil powers and restores God's dominion over Creation. It is somewhat surprising, therefore, to find that Paul does not pay more attention to the details of Jesus' activities and pronouncements during his earthly life. His Gospel does not give an account of Jesus' life.

Concerning his birth we learn nothing about its circumstances. Paul sets the stage for the salvation of humanity stating that God condemned sin in the flesh by "sending his own Son in the likeness of sinful flesh" (Rom. 8:3). This leaves a large gap in our understanding of his view of the incarnate Son. What, exactly, is "the likeness" of sinful flesh. Is Paul using this phrase echoing the words of God reported in *Genesis*, "Let us make man in our image, after our likeness" (Gen. 1:26)? No one understands this to mean that Adam and Eve were created gods. In other words, to be an image, or the likeness of God is not to be created a god. Similarly, to be in the likeness of sinful flesh is not to be sinful flesh. But, Paul insists, all humans are sinful flesh. Paul's use of the expression "the likeness of" may have been influenced by a very early hymn quoted by Paul. It says that a divine being took "the form of a servant, being born in the likeness of men" (Phil. 2:7). We may safely assume that for Paul "sinful flesh" and "men" are synonyms. On account of this equivocal phrasing about "the likeness" of sinful flesh or of men, through the centuries Christians have had strenuous debates about the "nature" of Jesus.

Paul sets out two things about Jesus "according to the flesh." He was a fellow Jew (Rom. 9:5), and a descendent of David (Rom. 1:3). As a Jew, he was "born under the law" (Gal. 4:4). The second piece of information would normally serve to establish Jesus' claim to being the Messiah. The first would indicate that he was a Jew expected to obey the law. That he was born under the law is preceded by the information that he was born of a woman, something that is universally the case of those born "according to the flesh," or as "sinful flesh," that is to say, as "men." This suggests that maybe the woman and the law are put together to confirm his being a Jew.

That Jesus was a descendent of David "according to the flesh," is contrasted to what he is according to the Spirit; he was "designated Son of God in power . . . by his resurrection from the dead" (Rom. 1:4). No doubt, in Paul's mind his birth in the Spirit as Son of God totally outshines his being a descendent of David born of a woman according to the flesh.

Jesus' birth, then, is not seen by Paul as one with special attributes, accompanied by memorable, supernatural events brought about by divine intervention. As both the gospels of Matthew and Luke report, Jesus was a descendent of David because he was the son of Joseph, his father. Paul does not take this to mean that he was the promised Messiah. The Messiah has no role to play in his theology. For him what counts is his having been raised from the dead and designated Son of God. He does refer to Jesus Christ, but in this construction "Christ," the Greek equivalent to the Hebrew word Messiah, is not a title but a last name, like Simon Peter, or Judas Iscariot. Thus, being born of a woman, born under the law and a descendent of David are all facts of life that belong to the life of Jesus "according to the flesh." His life on earth took place in the fallen world, before God made a new creation by the power of the Holy Spirit.

In a most revealing passage, Paul writes, "From now on, therefore, we regard no one from a human point of view [Greek:

according to the flesh]; even though we once regarded Christ from a human point of view [according to the flesh], we regard him thus no longer" (2 Cor. 5:16). Here Paul makes a significant confession while giving a very important piece of advice using himself as an example. As a result of the establishment of a new creation with the resurrection of Christ by the power of the Spirit, humans may live in either of two ecological systems. They may live "in the flesh" or they may live "in the Spirit," that is, "in Christ." Paul here says that Christians should see others as living in Christ, not as living in the flesh.

He then admits that at one time he saw Christ as one more human living in the flesh. This may be interpreted either as saying that he saw Jesus "according to the flesh," that is as no more than another human being, or as saying that the manner in which Paul considered Jesus was "according to the flesh," as the RSV translates "from a human point of view." In either case, looking at Jesus as no more than a human being or from a human point of view, Paul had become a persecutor of Christians. To the Galatians Paul writes, "you have heard of my former life in Judaism, how I persecuted the church of God violently and tried to destroy it" (Gal. 1:13). That is what he had done when he regarded Christ "according to the flesh." Seeing Christ as a human being, a fellow Jew with messianic illusions of grandeur who was crucified for sedition naturally drove him to persecute those who were now proclaiming him the promised Redeemer.

What he tells about the human Jesus can be presented in a short paragraph. From reading the four gospels we know that Jesus did many things. With any details, Paul only tells us about the institution of the bread and the wine as symbols of his body and blood. According to Paul, Jesus told his disciples to partake of these emblems often because by doing so they would be "proclaiming the Lord's death until he comes" (1 Cor. 11:23 – 26). Telling about this event in Jesus' life, Paul informs us that this took place "on the night when he was betrayed." This is all he reports about the passion, the trial, and the execution of Jesus: he was betrayed. When?, where?, by whom? Paul does not say.

It is quite reasonable to think that Paul knew about other things that Jesus had said and done. The oral traditions among the early Christians were quite rich, and Paul credits the oral tradition both for what he knows about the Last Supper and for the confession of faith that he quotes in 1 Corinthians 15:3 – 7. Here and there, Paul reports snippets from the tradition. For example, that Jesus "did not please himself" (Rom. 15:3), that he said, "no divorce" (1 Cor. 7:10), that "those who proclaim the gospel should get their living by the gospel" (1 Cor. 9:14). He also knew that Jesus had singled out the commandment to love (Rom. 13:9). It is quite amazing that Paul, the first Christian whose writings we possess, does not appeal to the oral tradition more often.

Paul also writes repeatedly of the crucifixion (Gal. 2:20; 2 Cor. 13:4; Phil. 2:8). As to who carried it out, Paul gives two answers. He attributes the action both to "the Jews" (1 Th. 2:14), and to the "rulers of this age" (1 Cor. 2:8). The assignment of blame for the crucifixion to "the Jews" is part of an amazing tirade against "the Jews" that is totally out of place, does not square with Paul's recognition that God's call to the Jewish people is "irrevocable" (Rom. 11:29), and is considered by most scholars as a non-Pauline interpolation added by a later hand, after Jews and Christians had parted company. His assertion that the crucifixion was brought about by the rulers of this age, that is to say by the principalities and powers, or elemental spirits of the cosmos who did not know "the wisdom of God," takes the crucifixion out of its historical setting and places it in a theological scenario that fits Paul's apocalyptic horizon. The rulers of the spheres are the agents of Satan, from whose power believers have been liberated by the power of the Spirit that raised Christ from the dead.

Of the historical life of Jesus, Paul singles out his obedience (Rom. 5:19) even unto death (Phil. 2:8), and his faith. For Paul Jesus did not live on earth with the advantages of a divine being. Jesus lived by faith. He faced the cross as a human who trusted the power of God. Unfortunately, translators have Paul writing about faith "in Jesus" when the Greek says "faith of Jesus." For example in the letter *To the Philippians*, Paul writes, "I have suffered the loss of all things, and count them as refuse, in order that I may gain Christ and be found in him, not having a righteousness of my own, based on law, but that which is through faith in Christ, the righteousness from God that depends on faith" (Phil. 3:8, 9). The Greek reads, in part, ". . . and be found in him, not having my own righteousness, that one coming from the law, but that one [righteousness coming] through the faith of Jesus, the righteousness coming from God based on faith." The righteousness coming from God, rather than the law, is based on the faith of Jesus. God raised Jesus from death on account of his faith. Believers who are justified by God, are justified because they "are found in him;" they live "in Christ" and benefit from his faith. Faith must have an object, and Paul is quite clear as to the only legitimate object of a Christian's faith: Christians have faith "toward God" (1 Th. 1:8).

Jesus' faith in God is what gives life to sinners. This point is made in another famous Pauline confession: "I have been crucified with Christ; it is no longer I who live, but Christ who lives in me; and the life I now live in the flesh I live by faith in the Son of God, who loved me and gave himself for me" (Gal. 2:20). This text says it best, but again attention must be paid to the original Greek, which reads: "but what I now live in the flesh, I live in the faith, that of the Son of God who loved me and gave himself for me." As a Christian Paul lives in two locations: "in the flesh" and "in the faith;" that is, Paul is crucified with Christ, and as a consequence the faith of the Son of God is active in Paul. Christians live "in Christ," as Paul does not tire to say. Paul does not have faith *in* Jesus. He has the faith *of* Jesus because he is "found in him." Jesus had faith in the effective power of God; likewise, Paul has the faith of Jesus in the power of God to raise the dead. In passing, it is also to be noted that in this very personal confession Paul gives specific credit to Christ saying that the Son of God "loved me and gave himself for me." It is not just that God loved the sinners, sent forth His Son, and pours out the Spirit on human hearts. It is also the case that the Son loves humanity and gave himself for all humans.

The obedience of Jesus Paul refers to, of course, was not obedience to the law that was "ordained by angels through an intermediary" (Gal. 3:19). Christ's obedience was the "obedience of faith" that made it possible for him to undergo a crucifixion trusting God. The obedience of faith that characterized the life of Jesus is the obedience to be observed in all those who, like Paul, have been crucified with Christ and live in the flesh *and* in the faith of Jesus. Thus, like the one in whom they live, Christians are also characterized by their faith and obedience. On that basis they receive the righteousness that has its source in God rather than the law.

Paul's main interest is in the story of the pre-existent divine being who eventually was "designated Son of God." To tell this story Paul relied on what is universally recognized as the words of one of the earliest Christian hymns. It was sung by Christians already by the middle of the first century. Here is a literal translation:

a. (Who) in form of God being
b. did not choose straining to be equal to God but emptied himself
c. form of Servant taking

II

a. In human likeness becoming
b. and found in human structures humbled himself
c. becoming obedient unto death

III

a. Therefore, even God above-exalted him
b. and granted him the name
c. which is above every name

IV

a. so that at the name of Jesus
b. every knee should bow in the heavens, the earth and the abyss
c. and every tongue confess: 'Lord Jesus Christ'

(Phil. 2:6 – 11)

It is not difficult to discern the dynamics of the hymn's content. Obviously the "therefore" at the beginning of the third stanza divides the hymn in two. The first two stanzas deal with the life of a divine being who died, and the last two contrast his life after his death with his original life. While the first and the third stanzas contrast two transitions, the second and the fourth take a closer look at the conditions that resulted from them.

Focusing on the first two stanzas, we note that the first begins and ends with a reference to "form," and the second does the same with the phrase "becoming." These stanzas have both parallels and contrasts. Existence in the form of god is contrasted with existence in the form of servant. Then, to become "in human likeness" is re-stated as being found "in human structures." Both stanzas begin with the preposition "in," and while the first says that he "emptied himself," the second parallels the idea saying that he "humbled himself."

These two stanzas work out the radical transition, from being divine with possibilities to ascend, to being human and reaching the lowest point. Considering who he was it is difficult to understand who he became. The unexpected transformation of his life, however, was not due to his "nature," but to a decision of his. The surprise element in this reversal is marked by the strongly adversative "but," (*alla* rather than *de* in the original Greek), before "emptied himself." Because of this decision he "was found" in the form of a human being in history, a being who is subject to death, and as such actually died. It would seem that the words "even death on a cross" are added by Paul to the original hymn to emphasize the thought that had caused him to quote the hymn in the first place.

The third and fourth stanzas emphasize parallelisms. The third begins and ends with "above," to underline that the final status was far superior to the one held before the decision to empty himself. The new condition is given special significance by pointing out that it was brought about by "even God." What unites these two stanzas is the concept of the name, which is mentioned three times. Moreover, the universality of the superior name in the third stanza is paralleled by the universality of the homage to the name in the fourth. That the two stanzas elaborate on a single idea is quite obvious: God has bestowed the title "Lord" on Jesus Christ, and as a consequence his exalted new status should be recognized by everyone throughout the three levels of the cosmos.

Something similar occurs in the first two stanzas except in the reverse. He who was in the form of god decided to make himself less rather than more and as a consequence ended up dead. While the first two stanzas show the movement from being to non-being, the last two show the movement from exaltation to worship. As a whole the hymn proclaims that the divine being, who decided to become less rather than to reach for a higher position in the chain of being, was exalted to an even higher position than the one he could have reached by himself. Being declared "Lord" by God was certainly far above being "in form of god."

To fully understand this early Christian view of Jesus Christ we must see it in terms of its intended upside-down anti-type. The decision of the pre-existent divine being to become less is being contrasted with the decisions of Eve and Adam to become more by eating the fruit offered by the serpent. According to the account in *Genesis,* the first couple was made "in the image of God" (Gen. 1:27); in this hymn the being in question is described as "in the form of God." Both descriptions make the point that these beings did not have to die, even if by nature humans were not immortal. Adam is specifically warned that his life depended on his obedience and that the day he should eat of the fruit of the forbidden tree he would die (Gen. 2:17; 3:3). Besides, when Adam and Eve do eat of the tree of the knowledge of good and evil, they do not lose an immortality which, in fact, they never had. They are barred from access to the tree of life, from whose fruit as mortals they depended in order to live. Desiring to be more than he was, that is, "equal to God" (Gen 3:5), Adam ate the forbidden fruit. As a result, he became less, a being who had to work the soil to sustain a life that would surely end in death. Straining to become more, Adam became a disobedient sinner. The contrast with the pre-existent being of the hymn could not be greater. Facing the temptation that pride offers, he decided to humble himself and be obedient. As a result he ended being far more than what he had been.

The argument of the hymn presupposes the notion of the chain of being, and the possibility for beings to climb or descend on the scale, thus becoming less or more. This notion was well established in Hellenistic culture. It classified beings according to the position they occupied in the hierarchy of being that started with inanimate objects and ascended all the way to the being of God. The being who was in the form of god occupied a position somewhere in the chain of being below God but above humans. Rather than to reach for a position higher in the chain, equal to God, he decided to descend to the position of human beings. As a result, he now occupies a position much higher up the chain than the one he originally had. He has been exalted by God above every other created being in the whole chain of being.

The theme of the hymn serves well the argument that Paul is making to his Philippian readers. He is advising them not to esteem themselves superior to others, but rather, in humility, to count others better than themselves. Here he offers them the being who made himself less, contrary to the human tendency to make oneself more, becoming a servant to others until death as the model to be imitated. To be noted is that the one who made the decision to become less and now occupies a position above every other created being is not a historical human being. The account of the sojourn in human form only dwells on his obedience to the will of God. Even if his human experience was an integral part of his trajectory from being in the form of god to being the Lord Jesus Christ before whom every knee should bow, it is not what the hymn emphasizes.

The Lord Jesus Christ of the hymn is the personification of the Pauline understanding of salvation, the prototype of those who, by means of the resurrection from the dead, attain to a condition "above" the one in which they now live. Choosing to become less in life is the way to become more. Further on in *To the Philippians*, Paul describes himself in the same terms. He who according to the law was "blameless" (3:6), came to consider such status as "refuse" (3:8) in order that he may know Jesus "and the power of his resurrection, and may share his sufferings, becoming like him in his death, that if possible I may attain the resurrection from the dead" (3:10 – 12). In Paul's vision, Jesus Christ is not the Last Adam because he came after the first Adam, or because another is not to come after him. He is the Last Adam because his "super-exaltation" to the Lord who is universally worshiped anticipates the glorification of all those who participate in his death and resurrection. Another way of saying it is that he is "the first-born among many brethren" (Rom. 8:29). He is the father of the race of those who by the power of the Gospel live "in the Spirit."

As noted earlier, at the end of the first section of the hymn Paul added the words "even death on a cross." These words appear to be his way of dramatizing the journey down the chain of being, for they give to the self-humbling of the divine being an even more tragic and incomprehensible twist. In the Roman world, it was very important to die well. There was a well-known protocol for a "noble death." Paul is referring to this when in the same letter, writing from prison and not knowing whether he will be set free or will be condemned to die, he says, "it is my eager expectation and hope that I shall not be at all ashamed, but with full courage now as always Christ will be honored in my body, whether by life or by death" (Phil. 1:20). To be afraid, rather than courageous facing death, was a very shameful thing. The "noble death" demanded courage and, of course, full command of what was happening. Roman citizens of rank were routinely given the right to choose the means by which to commit suicide, thus demonstrating control and courage. To die crucified was considered the most demeaning and shameful of deaths precisely because its cruelty made control and courage almost impossible. When the being who was in the form of god decided to make himself less rather than more, he could not have gone any lower than to die crucified.

At the end of the fourth stanza, Paul added another phrase to the hymn: "to the glory of God the Father." The second half of the hymn does set up the Lord Jesus Christ in a most enviable position. As the one who is above every other created being in the cosmos, it would appear that he has become the center of the universe. He is now the triumphant cosmic Lord. The second section of the hymn, however, does not credit the Lord Jesus Christ for the position he now occupies. He is the passive recipient and beneficiary of God's activity. Still, Paul felt that he had to put this full scenario in its proper perspective. The purpose of the trajectory of the one who ends up "above-exalted" is to bring glory to God. In Paul's universe, God is the one who is always and forever in control. Everything that happens is to bring about glory to Him. The salvation of humanity is the work of God. God is revealing his righteousness through Christ, who, on account of his faith and obedience, has been highly exalted and designated God's son. All living beings in the universe now owe him respect as their Lord on account of God's evaluation of his cosmic trajectory.

The modern popular preoccupation of Christians to establish a working relationship with Jesus as a friend is not something that Paul would understand. His concern is to live by the power of the Spirit that raised Christ as the Son of God and the Last Adam. It is as the first being of the new creation that Christ is also Lord, and all humans are his slaves who live by the same faith that sustained him even unto death. Their obedience of faith is patterned after the faith of Jesus in the justice of God.

VII God is Faithful

There is ample evidence that the Gospel preached by Paul was very upsetting to the early Christians, all of whom were Jews. Paul preached that the cross and the resurrection of Christ made it possible for human beings not to live under the power of sin, which had been the human condition since the Fall. The Jews who had been given the law as a means by which to "know sin" (Rom. 3:20), that is to identify transgressions as what unleashes the wrath of God (Rom. 4:15), understood that God's blessings and punishments were dependent on their fulfillment of the requirements of the law. To them, the notion that it was God's will that they no longer live under the law was beyond comprehension. Paul saw the law as having fulfilled its role during the period of Israel's childhood, a period in history that had come to an end with the death of Christ. The resurrection of Christ was a new creation which made it possible not to live under the law and the power of sin. As Paul explicitly says, "We are not under the law" (Rom. 6:15).

Jews saw themselves as being God's special people, the elect of God. Before their entry into the land of Canaan Moses had said to them, "You are a people holy to the Lord your God; the Lord your God has chosen you to be a people for his own possession out of all the peoples that are on the face of the earth" (Dt. 7:6). They had been told that the law had been given to them so they might attain to righteousness: ". . . it will be righteousness for us, if we are careful to do all this commandment before the Lord our God, as he has commanded us" (Dt. 6:25). The directive given to them was, "You shall therefore keep my statutes and my ordinances, by doing which a man shall live: I am the Lord" (Lev. 18:5). Besides, Moses had assured them that this would not be just a temporary arrangement: "Know therefore that the Lord your God is God, the faithful God who keeps covenant and steadfast love [*chesed*] with those who love him and keep his commandments, to a thousand generations . . . You shall be careful to do the commandments and the statutes and the ordinances, which I command you this day" (Dt. 7:9, 11). The setting up of the law and the covenant established a special relationship between God and the people. This arrangement, binding the people to obedience and to specific privileges, was central to the self-understanding of all Jews.

On the basis of this unique relationship, the prophet Zechariah told the Israelites: "He who touches you, touches the apple of his [God's] eye" (Zech. 2:8). By reason of his self-understanding, the Psalmist therefore pleaded, "Keep me as the apple of the eyes, hide me in the shadow of thy wings" (Ps. 17:8). The notion that the law was no longer at the center of their life with God, and that Jews as such were not occupying a special position before God, was anathema to most of Paul's fellow Christians.

To Paul the Christ event was not merely something that happened in history. It had been a cosmic turnover of the divine/human relationship. For him, it was essential to take this new reality into account. The mediator of the divine/human relationship was no longer the law, but the Christ who had come as the fulfillment of the promise. Thus, when Paul asks the question, "What then? Are we Jews any better off?" his immediate reaction is, "No, not at all" (Rom. 3:9). In this regard it may be noted that the gospel *According to John* also disassociates Christianity from the Jewish law. Throughout this gospel, Moses is credited with the giving of the law (Jn. 1:17; 7:19); Nicodemus and "the Jews" consider it "our law" (Jn. 7:51; 19:7); Jesus refers to it as "your law," and the narrator calls it "their law" (Jn. 8:17; 10:34; 18:31). In this gospel "the Jews" are a stereotype of the Christian Jews who have rejected the claim of divinity which the Johannine Christians are making for Jesus in the second half of the first century. As in the letters of

Paul, also in this gospel the Jews are charged with having the law but not keeping it. But, of course, there is a significant difference between the letters of Paul and the gospel *According to John*. Paul considers himself a good Jew, a son of Abraham of the tribe of Benjamin. He says "we" when writing about Jews. He insists that they are forever bound to God's purposes. The gospel *According to John*, to the contrary, reflects a situation in which Christians and Jews have definitely parted company and the Johannine community considers "the Jews" as the enemies of God.

Most Jews who heard Paul's Gospel apparently thought that if Paul was correct, God was not "the faithful God" they wished to worship. His word to them had become void; their claim to being the elect of God had turned out a lie. Given the choice between believing God's word to them and believing Paul's Gospel, it was obvious that Paul's word could not stand against God's. This was a very serious challenge that Paul could not ignore.

Paul preached a Gospel which demonstrated God's justice. Its core contained the vindication of God's faithfulness. The passages cited above from Deuteronomy and Leviticus bound God to the Jews and made their prosperity in the land dependent on their careful keeping of the law. Paul, however, sees God's faithfulness and salvation manifest in the fact that "the testimony of Christ was confirmed among you," the believers, since "you are not lacking in any spiritual gift, as you wait for the revealing of our Lord Jesus Christ; who will sustain you to the end, guiltless in the day of our Lord Jesus Christ, God is faithful" (1 Cor. 1:6 – 9). To let the charge that his Gospel made God unfaithful to the Jews go unchallenged was something Paul could not allow. In four of his letters he insisted that "God is faithful" (Rom. 3:3; 1 Cor. 1:9; 2 Cor. 1:18; 1 Th. 5:24). He wrote a long defense of God's faithfulness as part of the presentation of his Gospel in the letter *To the Romans*. It takes the whole of chapters nine through eleven.

To understand this most important section of the letter *To the Romans* there is nothing better than to follow closely its line of argument, even if this is at times a bit challenging.

The way he introduces the subject is quite revealing. He feels the need to make the point that what he is about to say is true. Claims to veracity often only serve to indicate that there is something under the table. Paul wants to make sure that his audience believes "that I have great sorrow and unceasing anguish in my heart. For I could wish that I myself were accursed and cut off from Christ for the sake of my brethren, my kinsmen by race" (Rom. 9:2 – 3). Apparently, Paul senses that his audience considers him a renegade Jew who is a traitor to his heritage; this audience is not predisposed to believe his concern for the Jews. To counter this misconception he lists the many ways in which his kinsmen, the Israelites, have been blessed over time. "To them belong the sonship, the glory, the covenant, the giving of the law, the worship, and the promises" (Rom. 9:4). This reinforces what he wrote earlier: "To begin with, the Jews are entrusted with the oracles of God" (Rom. 3:2). The things listed and the order in which they are listed is revealing. I would think that sonship here refers to their being the "children of God." The glory refers to the presence of God among them at Mt Sinai where the covenant and the law were given. The worship refers to the sacrificial system at the tabernacle and the temple. It may be a bit surprising to us that he does not refer to the temple directly, but this omission is consistent with Paul's vision. Not surprisingly he left for last what he considers most important, the promises.

A second list then adds, "to them belong the patriarchs, and of their race, according to the flesh, is the Christ" (Rom. 9:5). It is notable that he jumps from Abraham, Isaac and Jacob to Christ, overlooking Moses and David. But these three are "the patriarchs" who, at the end of his defense, he calls "the fathers" whose merit is a factor in God's faithfulness to Israel. For all these central elements of his heritage Paul blesses God who is over all. His defense of the faithfulness of God starts by praising God for what He has done for the Israelites. He felt the need to establish, first of all, that he had a great deal of admiration and thankfulness to God for Israel and its historical existence "in the flesh."

Having established his links to Israel, Paul states his counter claim: "But it is not as though the word of God had failed" (Rom. 9:6). This statement can only be understood as a correction of what some are saying concerning his preaching. This is marked by the "but" at the beginning. It points to the propagators of a misrepresentation of his Gospel. Anyone saying that Paul's God is an unfaithful God who does not keep his word to Israel is not representing Paul correctly.

Paul's defense of his God begins with an explication of the nature of election (Rom. 9:6 – 13). Have all the children of Abraham been among the elect? Certainly not. Ishmael and all his descendants and Esau and all his descendants were children of Abraham, but are not counted among the elect. This means that election is not something God did once for all and then continues automatically to include all the descendants of Abraham. Election is a dynamic process in time that is carried out by God according to His purpose, and it is activated by God's call, not by a person's genes. That is, election does not bind God to the past. God is always free to choose, a point that is made by the final quotation of the section. "As it is written, 'Jacob I loved, but Esau I hated.'" In other words, God is not bound by His election of Abraham. In reference to this declaration, it must be noted that in Hebrew usage "to love" and "to hate" may be used as synonyms, respectively, for "to choose" and "to not choose."

God's freedom to choose is understood by Paul, of course, within his apocalyptic symbolic universe. In such a universe absolute freedom is not a human attribute. God is the only one free. Humans live under beings who have power over them. The notion of the freedom of the will as a basic human attribute was introduced into Western theological discourse by St. Augustine toward the end of the fourth century C. E. It has not been part of Eastern theological discourse to this day. Augustine needed it in order to defend the notion that God did not create evil and that, therefore, evil does not exist. According to Augustine, evil takes place by the human misuse of the freedom of the will. When people make a wrong choice what they happen to choose is not itself evil. Choosing a lesser rather than a greater good in the chain of being is not a thing that exists, but an act of the will. Paul knew nothing about the freedom of the human will. In his apocalyptic universe God is the only one free, and he remains free especially when he exercises His power to elect.

In this context, then, Paul asks a rhetorical question. Is God's freedom to call the elect according to his purpose a cloak for injustice? (Rom. 9:14). Because of his understanding of justice, Paul can answer this question with a resounding "NO!" Justice is not something determined by moral reasoning or established by the law. Here Paul takes a quite radical break with the philosophical tradition. For Socrates, for example, justice is established by the law. The law cannot be disobeyed on account of it being unjust. The law reflects the convictions arrived at by reason and therefore it is just. For Paul, justice is what God in His freedom wills, not a written document. Human challenges to God's justice are misguided and unfruitful endeavors doomed to irrelevancy. God "has mercy on whomever he wills, and he hardens the heart of whomever he wills" (Rom. 9:18). Justice is what God does. The God of Paul is faithful because he is not bound by laws or by the past. His faithfulness is historically revealed; election is a process in history, and history is what takes place in an ever changing human horizon which is, at the moment, not completely under God's control.

This being the case, God is totally free to will what He chooses, and justice and faithfulness are not matters to be accounted in human terms. Paul has no trouble anticipating the logical rejoinder to this notion. "You will say to me then, 'Why does he still find fault? For who can resist his will?'" (Rom. 9:19). If God's will is totally free, and it operates in a different realm, God should not find fault with humans who do not obey his will when they are unable to guess what justice is. On what basis does God find humans at fault? Paul takes for granted God's freedom to act, and that his actions are just. This is at the core of the apocalyptic vision of reality. In this context Paul introduces the metaphor of the potter who uses clay to make vessels. To be kept in mind is that the metaphor is introduced to establish God's right to find fault even though justice is not determined by a written law. What the metaphor says is that a potter is free to use different portions of a lump of clay to make vessels according to his will, and that he is also free to change his mind while in the process of making a pot. Paul is making the point that what election shows is not that God finds fault with some people, but that God has always complete freedom to act and to change his mind.

At the core of Paul's defense of the faithfulness of God is his midrash on Jeremiah's visit to the potter's workshop (Rom. 9:22 – 24, on Jer. 18:1 – 11). Paul elaborates on two aspects of the story. One is that vessels for daily use have a limited shelf life. Their use will eventually wear them down, and they will end up in a shard heap. Vessels for "beauty" will be displayed in a prominent place in the house and will become family heirlooms. The point of Jeremiah's story is that the potter not only has power over the clay, he also has the freedom to change his mind as to what to do with the clay. Paul takes advantage of this and makes a second application. Vessels that are doomed to destruction, those not chosen, are not necessarily immediately destroyed. This gives Paul room to speculate that "God, desiring to show his wrath and to make known his power, has endured with much patience the vessels of wrath made for destruction, in order to make known the riches of his glory for the vessels of mercy, which he has prepared beforehand for glory, even us whom he has called, not from the Jews only but also from the Gentiles" (Rom. 9:22 – 24).

Paul redefines the vessels for daily use as vessels of wrath, and the vessels of beauty as vessels of mercy. It would appear that Paul is thinking of the coming *Parousia*, when those not elected will remain dead and those elected will make known the riches of God's glory. Leaving aside the vessels of wrath for now, it is important to note that Paul says "we" to identify himself with the Christians, not with his fellow countrymen the Jews. Christians, however, are being called from among both the Jews and the Gentiles. It is not the case that the Jews have been excluded. Therefore, it is true, as Paul claims, that the word of God has not failed the Jews.

That "we" Christians are made up of both Jews and Gentiles gives Paul the opportunity to point out that, as a matter of fact, the situation of the Jews who are not responding to God's call is not caused by God, but by themselves. While the Gentiles without seeking it are attaining God's righteousness, the Jews have failed to fulfill the law through which they have been trying to attain to righteousness. Thus they have stumbled over "the stumbling stone" (Rom. 9:32). The stone which God had placed for a stepping stone toward righteousness has turned into a stumbling stone to the Jews who "seeking to establish their own . . . did not submit to God's righteousness" (Rom. 10:3). In a pithy, somewhat awkward, statement he explains the problem the Jews had with the stone that caused them to stumble. "For Christ is the end of the law, that every one who has faith may be justified" (Rom. 10:4). The last part establishes the reason for the first part. God's purpose is to justify, and He justifies every one who has faith. Thus God no longer justifies on the basis of the law, but of the faith of Christ.

The first part has two words that are ambiguous: *end* and *law*. Does he mean end in terms of termination, or in terms of purpose or objective? It could be said that in either case the idea is unchanged if by *law* is meant the commandments, ordinances and statutes. That is, there is not much difference between saying that the objective of the law was to lead to Christ and saying that Christ put an end to the law's authority because once the objective or the goal has been achieved the law is no longer needed as the definer of transgressions. On the other hand, if by *law* is meant the whole of the Pentateuch, a usage well attested in Paul, then the notion that the Pentateuch has Christ as its objective, and that the Jews failed to read it properly, as he charges them in 2 Corinthians 3:15, is quite understandable. As he insists throughout, participating in the faith of Christ does not do away with the Pentateuch, the law, rather it "upholds the law" (Rom. 3:31) as the context within which to understands God's righteousness. At every step of the argument in these three chapters Paul cites a passage of Scripture as evidence supporting what he says, twenty four citations in all. There is no better way to uphold Torah than to make it the standard by which to evaluate what is being said.

As possessors of the Torah, the Jews should have been able to exercise faith and thereby attain God's righteousness. They stumbled, however, on the stone placed by God as a stepping stone because he was "the end" of the law, and they wished to continue trying to attain to righteousness on the basis of the law. The tragedy of the Jews was caused by their failure to realize that faith is submission to God's righteousness, acceptance of the purposes of God. God's purpose was to make Christ the means of righteousness to all those who believe in the one who raised him from the dead. The rest of Chapter 10, then, elaborates on the fact that the Jews "have a zeal for God, but it is not enlightened" (Rom. 10:2). Even though the opportunity to exercise faith is present, and doing so does not require impossible tasks, they have been refusing to believe. As a result, they have been a "disobedient and contrary people" (Rom. 10:21), as the prophet Isaiah had long ago declared.

Paul comes back to the topic at hand repeating the original rebuttal as a rhetorical question. "I ask, then, has God rejected his people? By no means! . . . God has not rejected his people whom he foreknew" (Rom. 11:1 – 2). This affirmation is based on a comparison between the present and the time of Elijah. Like Elijah, who was not the only Jew who worshiped Yahve, Paul is not the only Jew who "confesses with [his] lips that Jesus is Lord and believes in [his] heart that God raised him from the dead" (Rom 10:9). As in the time of Elijah seven thousand had not bowed their knee to Baal, "so too at the present time there is a remnant, chosen by grace. But it is by grace, it is no longer on the basis of works, otherwise grace would not be grace" (Rom. 11:5 – 6). Here Paul seems to realize that those seven thousand who had not bowed their knee to Baal had actually done something. Thus he writes that it is *no longer* by works, even if at one time it may have been. This is understandable when one considers that faith is the recognition and submission to

God as He acts in history. On this basis Paul could repeatedly say that salvation has always been attainable only by faith.

The wrong response to God's call, Paul goes on to explain, was caused by the fact that God actually elected some to attain what they sought and "hardened" others so as to fail to attain it. This description is dependent on the apocalyptic perspective where things are to be explained as fitting God's purposes. Paul elaborates it, appealing to the metaphor of their stumbling on the stone placed by God on Zion. Did they stumble so as to fall? (Rom. 11:11). Recalling Jeremiah's observation that the potter has the freedom to change his mind about what use to make of the clay, and the statement in Deuteronomy, "I will make you jealous of those who are not a nation" (Dt. 32:21), Paul suggests that the failure of "hardened" Jews is God's way of bringing salvation to the Gentiles, and to provoke jealousy on the part of the Jews. This maneuver on God's part is to be seen in terms of its outcome. Anticipating what he will say more explicitly a few lines below, Paul makes one of his classic *de minoris ad maiorem* arguments. "If their failure means riches for the Gentiles, how much more will their full inclusion mean" (Rom. 11:12), since their jealousy will bring them back to God. Paul later says, "as regards the gospel they are enemies of God, for your [the Gentiles'] sake, but as regards election they are beloved for the sake of their forefathers. For the gifts and the call of God are irrevocable" (Rom. 11:28 – 29). This is the ultimate answer to those who charge Paul with making God unfaithful to the Jews. It may also be noted that the notion of "the merits of the forefathers" was frequently appealed to by the Rabbis as the reason for God's continuous faithfulness to the Jews even when at times they did not deserve it.

Before making this ringing declaration, Paul elaborates on the strange ways in which God works, and, in the process, claims to be in possession of "a mystery" (Rom. 11:25). This section of the argument is an aside addressed to the Gentiles among his readers. To them he brings to mind an agricultural practice widely known. In order to prolong the productive life of olive trees, old branches were cut off and young branches from selected trees were grafted to the old roots. In this way it was avoided having to uproot old trees and wait years for newly planted trees to start producing fruit. Paul makes this illustration to remind the Gentiles that they are receiving their life as Christians from the ancient root that makes it possible for them to bear fruit. The "holy root" from which they as grafted branches receive energy and life is, of course, the ancient people of God, the Jews. This should prevent them from ever boasting. "Do not become proud, but stand in awe" (Rom. 11:20), he tells them. If you fail "to continue in God's kindness ... you too will be cut off" (Rom. 11:22). God is quite capable, just as He grafted you, to cut you off and "graft them [the Jews] again." Once again Paul uses a *de minoris ad maiorem* argument. "If you have been cut from what is by nature a wild olive tree, and grafted, contrary to nature, into a cultivated olive tree, how much more will these natural branches be grafted back into their own olive tree" (Rom. 11:24). Paul cannot give up on the eventual incorporation of the Jews back into God's people. (We may surmise that Paul has accommodated the allegory to his purpose and identifies the Gentiles as branches from "a wild olive tree." Most likely that is not what growers of olive trees used for grafts.) What the long argument has come up to is to affirm the eventual conversion of many Jews to the Gospel, thus demonstrating God's faithfulness to the Jews.

In Paul's time, a mystery was not something considered unsolvable. A mystery was a piece of information that is not generally available, but which is known by those to whom it has been revealed. Paul knows that "a hardening has come upon part of Israel, until the full number of the Gentiles come in, and so all Israel will be saved" (Rom. 11:25 – 26). Paul sees that at different times different people have been disobedient, but that is not their final status. "God has consigned all men to disobedience, that he may have mercy upon all" (Rom. 11:32). Paul consistently reserves for God the right to do His will, to punish and to save. Aware of this mystery, Paul can only break into an acclamation of "the depth of the riches and wisdom and knowledge of God! How unsearchable are his judgments and how inscrutable his ways!" (Rom. 11:33). Yes, God is faithful, and his purposes are accomplished according to his foreknowledge. To human beings, however, God's ways are beyond their capacity to understand. In this Paul follows the Wisdom tradition. According to it, God "has made everything beautiful in its time, also he has put eternity into man's heart, yet so that he cannot find out what God has done from the beginning to the end" (Eccl. 3:11). "God is in heaven, and you upon earth; therefore let your words be few" (Eccl. 5:2).

As already noted, Paul sees things primarily in terms of the apocalyptic symbolic universe within which he lived. It is not a question of finding out the reason for God's decisions in human experience and explaining God's activity in terms of human decisions. It is not the case that God finds fault in humans and reacts. It is that God acts according to his own purposes. He takes the initiative in all his actions. He is in command. Righteousness is what God does. Humans need to recognize the rights of the Creator God to act. Creatures do not cause the Creator to act. Even though the apocalyptic vision affirms the Fall of humanity under the power of Satan, what apocalypticism aims to make clear is that God is sovereign and his ultimate triumph is certain. Thus, the rule of Satan over the fallen world is not to be given ultimate significance, especially after the death of Christ on the cross and the New Creation brought about by the raising of Christ to glory. In this symbolic universe God is ultimately in control and everything takes place according to his designs. In an apocalyptic universe God's foreknowledge and purposes are sovereign. Predestination is an undisputed part of it.

As noted, Paul is also influenced by the Wisdom tradition that insisted on coming to terms with the limitations of the human capacity to explain God's ways. In his defense of God's faithfulness, however, he falls into the trap of explaining the immediate situation by making God do things to provoke the Jews to jealousy, a rather questionable tactic. Still, his dependence on the Wisdom tradition seems to have been what kept Paul from the kind of apocalyptic descriptions of the battles between good and evil using ancient creation mythologies to elaborate on the cosmic wars that will eventually end with the triumph of God over Satan. Such elaborate descriptions of the ultimate battles between Christ and Satan abound in the apocalyptic literature of the time, but are noticeably absent in the writings of Paul.

It must be recognized that historical Christianity found Paul's argument too radical. As pointed out in my short review of it, even if one adopts Paul's apocalyptic point of view, the transitions in the argument are fragile. He finds himself in a real dilemma because on the one hand he denies that God had rejected the Jews, but on the other he thinks the apocalyptic turning of the ages had taken place and a new creation has been established in which the old arrangements no longer hold. Thus he saw that salvation no longer depended on obedience to the commandments of the law of Moses. Christianity took the position that the law of the ten commandments written on stone tablets is still operative, something that Paul explicitly rejects (2 Cor. 3:3). On the other hand, it proclaimed that God had rejected the Jews as the chosen people, consigning them to perdition and becoming a religion of Gentiles. Thus, while at the beginning of the second century Christianity affirmed that God had rejected the Jews, at the middle of the first century Paul had developed a long argument to defend himself from charges that his Gospel taught that. Paul's Gospel saw all human beings, Jews and Gentiles, on an equal footing, and Christian Jews objected to that. They could not accept Paul's Gospel of God's impartiality (Rom. 2:11). To them God's impartiality meant that God was being unfaithful to the Jews. Historical Christianity also rejected God's impartiality by condemning the Jews to perdition.

Today some may find Paul's apocalyptic universe at worst theologically flawed or, at best, theologically unappealing. If that is the case, what course is to be taken by those who still believe in God's faithfulness? It must be recognized that Paul's universalistic opening of the Gospel is also indebted to his apocalypticism. Paul' apocalypticism, as noted above, is quite restrained. His defense of

God's faithfulness is to be understood as faithful to his purpose in creation. It would seem to me that the correct response to Paul's apocalyptically framed argument is not to try to cram ourselves into Paul's symbolic universe where God works his way according to his foreknowledge and humans cannot change his course of action. For one thing, the apocalyptic is not the only biblical symbolic universe. Indeed, in the gospel *According to John* apocalypticism is explicitly rejected, and Satan, an indispensable protagonist in apocalypticism, is said to be the "father of lies" (Jn. 8:44). In other words, as Karl Barth liked to point out, his existence is a lie.

The task facing anyone believing in God's faithfulness is to transpose the Gospel of God's righteousness to our own symbolic universe, one in which God's calls "according to his purpose" are displayed not only in human history, where there is a continuous display of the work of the Spirit who gives eternal life to believers, but also in the process of creation that is taking place continuously in the stars of the heavens and in the animals and the vegetation of the earth. To believe in God's faithfulness is to be open to the working of the Holy Spirit who is active in the *creatio continua* taking place in nature, and is consummating the New Creation in the lives of believers. Today God's faithfulness is to be seen in an even broader universal horizon than the apocalyptic one that informed Paul's understanding of God's activity.

VIII By Which Law?

Paul demonstrates his mental agility in many ways; one of these, as we had the opportunity to see already, is his use of rhetorical questions that engage and challenge his audience to think, to consider and to evaluate what he is saying. The rhetorical question of the title above opens an important window into Paul's mind. It allows us to see that more than one law plays a role on his theological horizon. The answer given by Paul to this question identifies two: the law of works and the law of faith.

The translators of the RSV took advantage of the semantic range of the word law (*nomos*) in Greek. They have translated the verse: "Then what becomes of our boasting? It is excluded. On what principle [*nomos*]? On the principle [*nomos*] of works? No, but on the principle [*nomos*] of faith" (Rom. 3:27). This suggests that the Greek word *nomos*, which is most often translated "law," can also mean "that which has authority." This meaning has been rendered rather narrowly here as "principle." The Greek word normally refers to the Torah, the five books traditionally assigned to Moses the law giver or, in an even broader way to what Paul calls "the Scriptures" (Gal. 3:22), which includes the Pentateuch, the Prophets, and the Psalms. The Jews also called the whole of their scriptures the Torah.

Without being specific, Paul say, "I delight in the law of God" (Rom. 7:22). By contrast, he says that "the mind that is set on the flesh is hostile to God; it does not submit to God's law, indeed it cannot" (Rom. 8:7). Besides "the law of God," the apostle also mentions "the law of the Spirit of life in Christ Jesus" which has set him free from "the law of sin and death" (Rom. 8:2). He then elaborates, without specifying which law he has in mind, that there is something which "the law, weakened by the flesh," cannot do (Rom. 8:3). Reading on, we learn that what the law could not do was give life to those who live under the power of sin in a fallen creation. The paragraph culminates with the affirmation that "he who raised Jesus Christ from the dead will give life to their mortal bodies through the Spirit which dwells in them" (Rom. 8:11), that is, to the bodies of those who believe in the One who raised Jesus Christ. The law is unable to give life because, as Paul intimates in a contrary to fact conditional sentence, it was not given through Moses for that purpose (Gal. 3:21).

To make the issue a bit more confusing, Paul also says that his rule in all the churches is, "Let everyone lead the life which the Lord has assigned to him, and in which God has called him" (1 Cor. 7:17). This means that it makes no difference whether a person was circumcised or uncircumcised when becoming a Christian. Neither condition counts in favor or against him. The only thing that counts is "keeping the commandments of God" (1 Cor. 7:19). This raises the question of which commandments Paul has in mind. He has just said that all that is required is to lead the life assigned by the Lord according to the condition in which each one is found when called. He also says that every Christian whose mind has been renewed by the Spirit is able to determine what is the will of God (Rom. 12:2). Are we to assume that the minds that are led by the Spirit attain knowledge of God's commandments and observe them?

In light of the evidence, it is not surprising that there have been those who think that Paul contradicts himself when writing about the law. On the one hand, he says that "the law is holy, and the commandment is holy and just and good" (Rom. 7:14). On the other, he says that the chain that drags men and women into a hopeless death is made of two links: law and sin (1 Cor. 15:56). More to the point, he firmly aligns the law with the wrath of God, rather than with God's righteousness (Rom. 4:15).

While fully cognizant of the wide semantic range of the word *nomos* and of his references to several laws, we may begin to come to a better understanding of Paul's theology by taking into account the basic function of the law in the lives of Jews in Paul's time. The most immediate practical role of the law was as the institution separating Jews from Gentiles. It placed a special distinguishing mark on Jews. They were the ones bound to God by a covenant with the law at its core. That the law had been given to them was the mark of their status as the elect of God; therefore, Gentiles were neither expected nor able to observe it. The law established and maintained the Jewish way of life. As the boundary marker it made intercourse between Jews and Gentiles almost impossible in any meaningful personal way, even if social and commercial transactions were the order of the day between them. The law provided the Jews their ecological environment, and kept them apart.

It must be recognized, however, that the centrality of the law in the lives of Jews was a rather recent development. After the Exile (605 – 538 B.C.E.), the Jews sought to reorganize their lives as a nation with a reconstructed temple in Jerusalem where Yahve, the only true God, was recognized. At that time their priests edited the Pentateuch, and the Torah became the authoritative code for their theocratic commonwealth. Political, social, economic and religious life was now to be lived according to the law.

After the Exile, Jews lived not only in Palestine; they were dispersed throughout the Fertile Crescent, from Babylon to Egypt, from Palestine to Spain and beyond. Not long after the Exile the actual origins of the Pentateuch were forgotten and the Jews accepted the Torah, now ascribed to Moses, as of divine origin. When Alexander the Great (333 – 312 B.C.E.) united the Mesopotamian and the Mediterranean worlds into one civilization with Hellenistic culture as the unifying factor, the Jews began to find ways to adjust the laws of Torah to the new circumstances of life in an urban Hellenistic environment. The flourishing of Jewish life in Alexandria prompted the translation of the Torah into Greek beginning in the first half of the second century B.C.E., and the Septuagint, as this translated Torah came to be called, became the Jewish Scripture in most synagogues of the Hellenistic world. Philo of Alexandria, the most prominent Jewish contemporary of Jesus and Paul, makes clear that the wisdom of the Torah was considered by Jews to be far superior to the teachings of the Greek philosophers. Thus, it gave the Jews a strong sense of identity and of religious superiority in the Roman Empire.

No Jew would deny the wisdom of Torah, or disavow its validity. Neither did Paul. When arguing for the universality of God's promise to Abraham, and that all those who like Abraham have faith in God are justified before God, Paul asks rhetorically, "Do we then overthrow the law by this faith? By no means! On the contrary, we uphold the law" (Rom. 3:31). For that to be the case, Paul must have in mind more than one way of seeing the authority of the law, or the way it functions.

To make sense of Paul's references to "the law," "the law of God," "the other law in my members," "the law of my mind," "the law of Christ," "the law of works," "the law of sin," and "the law of faith" one must notice that while some designations may be different ways of referring to the same thing, not all of them can be interpreted in this way. Thus, it may be helpful to begin by aligning some of the phrases that do seem to refer to the same thing. I would think that the law of God and the law of Christ are the same. Since Paul says that he delights in the law of God "in his inmost self," it is reasonable to think that the "the law of my mind" also refers to the same law (Rom. 7:22, 23). He makes these statements when detailing the inner struggle of the Christian who still lives in the flesh after becoming a new creation by receiving the Spirit. The struggle has to do with the inability to do the good he wishes to do and the propensity to do the evil he does not wish to do. Continuing this reasoning he says, "So I find it to be a law that when I want to do right, evil lies close at hand" (Rom. 7:21). We now have three laws at play: 1) the law of God to which he agrees in his inmost self, 2) the law in his members which would seem to be his natural inclination not to do what his mind tells him to do, and 3) the law that activates an interior struggle between the two laws operating in him. Thus, even though he delights in the law of God, which is the law in his mind, he has another law in his members at war with the law in his mind. He ends admitting that "I of myself serve the law of God with my mind, but with my flesh serve the law of sin" (Rom. 7:25). In summary, Paul finds himself dealing with two laws: the law of God, of Christ, of his mind, of faith, and the law of sin, of his members, of the flesh, of works. The law that causes these two laws to conflict operates only on those who, like Paul, delight in the law of God.

It appears to me that the best way to make sense of all these statements of Paul is to recognize that Paul has radically redefined the human predicament of living in a fallen creation. He has done this through his understanding a) that the death of Christ on the cross put an end to the absolute power of the law as the judge of sins, and b) that the resurrection of Christ by the power of the Spirit now empowers those who believe in the God who raised Christ to be free from the power of sin and the law. Their lives are now empowered and guided by the Spirit. Against those who live thusly, Paul says, "there is no law" (Gal. 5:23).

Prior to the new creation in Christ, the whole of humanity lived in slavery to powers Paul calls the "elemental spirits of the universe" (Gal. 4:3, 9). The Greek noun, *stoicheia*, here translated "elemental spirits," basically means "elements." The word defines the basic components in a system. Thus we have the 118 elements in chemistry, letters of the alphabet as the elements of a language, and the notes of the scale as the elements of music. To know what Paul means by the "elements of the universe" to which all humanity is enslaved prior to the death and resurrection of Christ, we depend on the phrase by which Paul described them: "beings that by nature are no gods" (Gal. 4:8). These are the beings that operate in the spheres of the chain of being that separates the fallen creation from its creator God. To them Paul assigns responsibility for the crucifixion of Jesus (1 Cor. 2:8).

Bondage to the *stoicheia* was experienced by both Jews and Gentiles prior to their faith in Christ. To the Christians at Rome Paul wrote, "we are discharged from the law, dead to that which held us captive" (Rom. 7:6). When Paul says, "so with us, when we were children, we were slaves to the elemental spirits of the universe" (Gal. 4:3), he is referring to himself and all fellow Jews who lived in bondage under the law even though at the time they knew the true God. He completes the description referring to the Gentiles by saying, "when you did not know God you were in bondage to beings that by nature are no gods" (Gal. 4:8). Paul could see himself and his fellow Jews enslaved to elemental spirits only from hindsight, after having experience the liberating power of the Gospel. One of the "elements" that had enslaved Jews, and still enslaves those who refuse to believe in the Gospel, is the law. It is the prison that keeps Jews locked in (Gal 3:23). From a Christian perspective, life as a Jew under the law of Moses and life as a Gentile without this law is life in bondage to *stoicheia,* elemental spirits. Within the fallen creation, as an "elemental power" controlling Jewish life, the law had become detached from the being of God. The giving of the law had been through an intermediary, Moses, and it had been "ordained by angels" (Gal. 3:19). Because of this, Paul says, "I through the law died to the law, that I might live to God" (Gal. 2:19). In this short sentence Paul uses the same word to refer to two different things. In other words, Paul says that the Torah told him that he had to make a choice between God and the law of Moses, and he had decided to disengage himself from the law, to die to it, in order to live attached to God.

Paul sees the law as having served Israel through its childhood period. From the time it was given at Sinai to the time when it reached its goal, the death and the resurrection of Christ (Rom. 10:4), the law fulfilled a legitimate and necessary function. Paul characterizes it by the metaphor of the *paidagogos,* the slave in Hellenistic upper class households who was in charge of supervising the activities of children during their waking hours. He was to make sure that they were where they were supposed to be, did

Meditations on the Letters of Paul

not do what they were not supposed to do, and fulfilled the tasks they had been assigned. This "custodian" was responsible for the safety and well-being of the children under his charge. He was not their tutor or teacher. When the children were with their tutor, the *paidagogos* was having a break. Once a child reached the age the father had established, he could go about town alone, as an adult, without being escorted by his *paidagogos*.

Paul uses the metaphor of *paidagogos* to make an important clarification. "So the law was our custodian until Christ came . . . . But now . . . we are no longer under a custodian; for in Christ Jesus you are all sons of God, through faith . . . . I mean that the heir, as long as he is a child, is no better than a slave . . . he is under guardians and trustees until the date set by the father. So with us; when we were children, we were slaves to the elemental spirits of the universe. But when the time had fully come, God sent forth his son, . . . to redeem those who were under the law, so that we might receive adoption as sons . . . . So through God you are no longer a slave but a son, and if a son then an heir" (Gal. 3:24 – 4:7). Those in Christ, he says, are the heirs promised by God personally to Abraham 430 years before the giving of the law through Moses (Gal. 3:15 – 18).

Metaphors are very useful to expand the horizons of the imagination. Paul uses the metaphor of the *paidagogos* to contrast the situation of a child who is under a custodian to that of an adult who moves about in freedom. He expands the horizon by pointing out that heirs while under a custodian are no better than slaves of the household. Then, he shifts gears to contrast the situation of the slave to that of the redeemed former slave. Finally, he applies the expanded metaphor to contrast the Jew who is under the law with the person who, as a believer in the One who raised Christ from the dead, is a redeemed son and full heir of the riches of God. Christians, in other words, are not children under a *paidagogos* but adults with freedom of movement and new responsibilities. Christians are not "under the law" (Rom. 6:15).

Besides recognizing the historical function of the law as the custodian during the period of childhood, that is, from Sinai to Golgotha, Paul also thinks that the law has a psychological function. Since Adam, all humans live in a fallen creation and they, even before the entrance of the law at Sinai, sinned and died because of their sinning (Rom. 5:12). Living without a law they may be under the illusion that they are not sinners. Sin, however, is carrying on its deadly work in them. A very important function of the law is to objectify sins, to make sin sinful. Paul says that "the law came in to increase the trespass (Rom. 5:20), that is, to identify transgressions as sin (Gal. 3:19). Ultimately, he says, "if it had not been for the law, I should not have known sin" (Rom. 7:7).

The law not only exposes the sinful nature of specific activities which are now defined as transgressions (Gal. 3:19). It also "awakens" the person to reveal the "dormant" evil inside. Apart from the law the person feels healthy and prosperous. The coming of the commandments, however, brings death with it. "For sin, finding opportunity in the commandment, deceived me and by it killed me" (Rom. 7:10). The entrance of the law, therefore, not only exposes the existence of transgressions; it also gives sin the opportunity to deceive and by means of the law to kill. Given human nature, the law's command not to do this or that, awakens the desire to try these things. In this way the law makes human beings accountable for their actions, and thereby subjects them to the penalties of the law. "For the law brings wrath, but where there is no law there is no transgression" (Rom. 4:15). It may be said that as the custodian of children the law plays a positive role in the life of Israel. However, as the arbiter of sins, the revealer of dormant evil, and the energizer of God's wrath it certainly functions negatively. It is the agent of death and has nothing to do with the salvation of humanity.

Paul's greatest struggle with his fellow Christians was centered on their insistence that obedience to the commandments of the Sinai law was the path to life. Paul could not agree. The path to life was traced by the cross and the resurrection of Christ. Those walking on it were being led by the Spirit according to the ultimate will of God. As Paul pointedly says, "If you are led by the Spirit you are not under the law" (Gal. 5:18). Since the Spirit has made them new creatures and has renewed their minds, they are able to determine by themselves what is God's will. They serve the law of God in their inmost selves. The problem with the law given by Moses is that "it does not rest on faith" (Gal. 3:12). It demands "works."

Paul becomes quite frustrated and gets angry with the Galatians who had accepted his preaching of the Gospel and then, advised by other Christian apostles who said that Paul was wrong and that they were supposed to become keepers of the law and "live like Jews," decided to accept this other "gospel" and were about to become circumcised. This was to Paul the most obnoxious negation of the Gospel. To the Galatians he writes, "You are severed from Christ, you who would be justified by the law; you have fallen away from grace" (Gal. 5:4). This is a very serious indictment of those who wished to live under the law. Earlier in the letter, however, he had pointed out a more drastic conclusion to the argument of those other apostles who had perturbed the Christian experience of the Galatians. Its force is an argument *reductio ad absurdum*: "if justification were through the law, then Christ died to no purpose" (Gal. 2:21). This is the crux of the theology of Paul. To imagine that the crucifixion of Christ was the execution of a person charged with sedition was obscene. The crucifixion was followed by a resurrection, and they were both acts of God that brought about the possibility to live no longer in slavery to the law of works but in the freedom of the power of the Spirit. To seek righteousness by means of the law was to deny that the cross of Christ had accomplished a cosmic transformation by the creation of life "in the Spirit." Living in Christ does not empower Christians to keep the law of Moses that marks frontiers and puts confidence in the flesh. It empowers Christians to find delight in the law of God that the mind renewed by the New Creation agrees to. Unlike the law of Moses which awakens dormant sin, this law brings peace, love and joy.

IX ALL HAVE SINNED

It seems that every culture, even the earliest ones we know about, is aware that there is something wrong in the human person. This "something wrong" is identified differently and understood to have come about in different ways. Most ancient stories of creation include a detail that expresses the culture's understanding of this universal characteristic in human beings. For example, The *Enuma Elish*, the Babylonian creation story, says that humans were created because the gods needed servants. To give them life the gods used the blood of Kingu, the lover of Tiamat, the mother of the gods. He was chosen because he was guilty of starting the rebellion against Apsu, Tiamat's husband and head of the pantheon. Having been created with the blood of the "guilty one," human beings now have a flaw in their makeup.

The story of creation found in Genesis 2:4 – 3:24, which makes the point that human beings were created to obey God, locates the problem in the human desire to become "more." Faced with a conflict of interests Eve and Adam decided to assert their independence rather than to remain obedient. Their action brought about an immediate divine reaction. They were expelled from the Garden of Eden, denied access to the tree of life, and condemned to labors peculiar to each. The Hebrew language has four words to describe the actions that demonstrate that something is wrong in the human constitution. The four are used by the Psalmist in a short poem: "Blessed is he whose transgression is forgiven, whose sin is covered. Blessed is the man to whom the Lord imputes no iniquity, and in whose spirit there is no deceit" (Ps. 32:1 – 2).

Transgression, sin, iniquity and deceit, as the words have been translated into English, are the manifestations of what is wrong in the human personality. The roots of the Hebrew words refer, respectively, to stepping out of bounds, missing the mark, being crooked, and being vacuous. The first two describe actions, and the last two describe conditions. If the desired opposites are to be attained, the person should keep within the boundaries, hit the mark, be straight, and have substance. These words show how the "something" that is wrong in human beings came to be understood with the passage of time.

It would seem that originally sin had to do with failing to observe the limit between the sacred and the profane. Such failing produced a stain that rendered the person impure or unclean. This situation required the offering of a sacrifice to regain purity. Depending on the way in which the sacred had been polluted or why it needed to be restored, different sacrifices were specified as necessary. In ancient Israel, besides the evening and morning offerings and the ones connected to specific festivals and the Sabbath, there were sin offerings, burnt offerings and peace offerings required to establish or regain ritual purity (Lev. 9).

In the Old Testament there is no sacrifice prescribed for the transgression of one of the Ten Commandments. The understanding of sin in reference only to the distinction between the sacred and the profane is tied to the understanding that the way to live a good life is related primarily to nature, and that divine power is present in specific things, places and times. Human beings must live conscious of how they behave in reference to them. To be in favor with God, human beings must respect the boundary between the profane and the sacred. In the case of an infraction, they are to get right with God at the altar of sacrifice.

The prophets brought about a significant shift when they insisted that what the people did at the altar of sacrifices was annulled by their conduct with their neighbors, not only by profaning sacred things. They preached that God is disgusted with the smell of burnt offerings and sin offerings from people who take advantage of the weak, the poor, the widows and the orphans. In doing so, they transferred the arena where the human divine relationship may be broken from nature to history — from actions that fail to respect distinctions between sacred and profane objects to actions that fail to respect one's neighbors. Sin has to do with questions of justice, compassion and peace in the community (Am. 5:21 – 24; 8:4 – 6; Mic. 3:1 – 4; 6:11 – 14; Jer. 6:20, 8:10).

With the reforms of King Josiah and the appearance of the book now known as *Deuteronomy* and the ministry of the prophet Jeremiah shortly before the Exile, the establishment of the Second Temple after the return from the Babylonian Exile, and the editing of the Pentateuch as the Torah, the Jewish people reached a new plateau in their religious development. Many things in their understanding of their life with God were re-defined, and sin became the transgression of the law. After the Exile, Jews were dispersed throughout the Fertile Crescent and the Mediterranean basin and, therefore, access to the temple in Jerusalem became problematic for many. A new institution, the synagogue, did not take the place of the temple, but it fostered the study of the Torah and prayer as valid substitutes for animal sacrifices. In this new environment, Torah became the umbilical cord of the human divine relationship. Judaism became the religion of only one God, Yahve, and of obedience to Yahve's law. In the Diaspora, where Jews lived in constant contact with Gentiles, Torah became the identity badge of Jews.

Paul was a Jew reared in the Judaism of Torah. He knew quite well that according to the Jews sin is the transgression of the law: "where there is no law, there is no transgression" (Rom. 4:15). Or, "through the law comes knowledge of sin" (Rom. 3:20). The possession of the law gave Jews their identity and a sense of privilege before God. They were exceptional, not Gentile sinners (Gal. 2:15). Paul begins his exposition of God's faithfulness and justice establishing that God does not have favorites (Rom. 2:11). The argument starts by pointing out that Gentiles who do not see fit to honor God, even though God's eternal power and deity are plainly visible in creation, are being punished by God. Moreover, "though they know God's decree that those who do such things deserve to die, they not only do them but approve those who practice them" (Rom. 1:20, 32). Paul is aware that "my brethren, my kinsmen by race" would have no difficulty recognizing the justice of God that punishes Gentile sinners. What must have surprised his brethren is Paul's assertion that these Gentiles "know God's decree." This affirmation is referred to later in the argument when Paul writes that "Gentiles who have not the law do by nature what the law requires" (Rom. 2:14). This indicates that Paul does not agree with the Jews who think that all Gentiles are sinners. If sin is understood to be the transgression of the law, some Gentiles are sinners while others are not. In this context it is clear that Paul is being sarcastic when he addresses an imaginary Jew and asks him, "But if you call yourself a Jew and rely upon the law and boast of your relation to God and know his will and approve what is excellent, because you are instructed in the law, and if you are sure that you are a guide to the blind, a light to those who are in darkness, a corrector of the foolish, a teacher of children, having in the law the embodiment of knowledge and truth — you then who teach others, will you not teach yourself?" (Rom. 2:17 – 21). This rhetorical tour de force describes everything wrong with the prevailing Jewish self-understanding as privileged non-sinners. Paul makes the point explicitly: their claims to have "the written code and circumcision" as safeguards is negated by their consistent breaking of the law (Rom. 2:27).

In this context, Paul again defends himself from the charge that he is a purveyor of sinfulness because he fails to observe and approves others who fail to observe the Jewish purity laws. Paul is defending God's justice. His opponents charge that he is lying by denying that the law is the instrument of God's justice. He therefore asks with an ironic tone, "But if through my falsehood God's truthfulness abounds to his glory, why am I still being condemned as a sinner?" (Rom. 3:7). To prove that what he asserts is not a falsehood but God's truth, that is, that as a matter of fact Jews are not at all better off before God, he quotes Palms 14, 53, 5, 140, 10, 36, and Isaiah 59. He restates the claim: "I have already charged that all men, both Jews and Greeks, are under the power of sin" (Rom. 3:9). Of crucial significance is that he does not say "under the law," in which case the law would continue to be of central significance and justification would be by "works of law." This Paul specifically denies (Rom. 3:20). Instead of "under the law," very intentionally Paul wrote "under the power of sin."

This distinction is crucial to Paul. To the Jews, who still live under the law, sin is the transgression of the law. Of course, since ignorance of the law is no excuse, Gentiles are almost by necessity sinners. Paul, as I have argued already, is an apocalypticist for whom the notion of the Fall is central. The notion of the Fall does not merely claim that human beings no longer live in Eden. The Fall means that humans now live under "the god of this world." The Fall has had cosmic consequences and one of the most obvious ones is that humans live under the power of sin. This is true, as Paul insists, for everyone, both Jews and Gentiles who live in "this present evil age." Paul personifies sin as a cosmic power. With the sin of Adam and Eve, "sin came into the world. . . sin indeed was in the world before the law was given" (Rom. 5: 12 – 13). By the power of sin "death reigned" over all men and women because all of them sin (Rom. 5:17).

Paul's argument is that sin cannot be limited to the transgression of the law because there was sin and death from Adam to Moses, before the law entered the picture (Rom. 5:14). In another context, Paul asks rhetorically, "Are we to sin because we are not under law but under grace? By no means!" (Rom. 6:15). If sin is the transgression of the law, and we are not under law, sinning should not be possible. For Paul sinning is very much possible because everyone who lives in the flesh is under the power of sin. The same point is made by saying that "apart from the law sin lies dead. I was once alive apart from the law, but when the commandment came, sin revived and I died" (Rom. 7:9). The law arouses sinful passions that were there all along (Rom. 7:5). The notion that the law revives or awakens dormant sin can only be understood when sin is conceived as something much broader than what is condemned by the law. Within Paul's apocalyptic horizon sin is a cosmic power which came into the world with the Fall. It is much more than just transgression of the law. The law makes sin "countable" (Rom. 5:13); it makes it a "transgression." It "came in to increase the trespass" (Rom. 5:20), but, it does not cover the whole of its reality.

Paul is writing, however, not as an apocalyptic Jew, but as an apocalyptic slave of Christ. As such, he no longer lives only in the flesh, in a mortal body, under the power of sin and under the law. He is a new creation in Christ. He lives in the Spirit, as a member of the body of the Risen Christ by the power of the Spirit. He is no longer under the law of sin, but under grace. In the new creation sin is seen from a different perspective because in it the law no longer establishes the relationship with God and the power of sin is not operative. In the new creation those who live in Christ have been freed from sin and from the law. For them, the law is no longer an instrument of condemnation (Rom. 8:1).

Living in Christ is living by faith. It is living "transformed by the renewal of your mind, that you may prove what is the will of God, what is good and acceptable and perfect" (Rom. 12:2). As argued in a previous meditation, Paul understands that Christians who live by the power of the Spirit who raised Christ from the dead have a mind renewed by the Spirit that makes them capable of discerning spiritual things. They are expected to assume responsibility for their lives; this much is concomitant to having freedom in Christ. They are empowered to determine what is good and acceptable and perfect in the sight of God. They must now lead their lives according to the Spirit and be fully convinced that their conduct is a demonstration of the love that God has poured into their hearts. To live this way is the obedience of faith, which is quite other than the obedience of the works of law. In the context of the Christians whose lives are "a fragrant offering, a sacrifice acceptable and pleasing to God" (Phil. 4:18), Paul defines sin in yet another way. In the case of Christians who live by their obedience of faith, "whatever does not proceed from faith is sin" (Rom. 14:23).

Meditations on the Letters of Paul

This definition is dependent on Paul's understanding of the obedience of faith. If faith is a way of being empowered by the Spirit that produces the fruit of the Spirit and allows the mind to discern the will of God, then it is quite logical to define sin as that which does not proceed from faith. According to him, even though Christians still live in bodies of flesh they live in the Spirit as creatures of the new creation. They no longer live under the law. Therefore, Paul does not tell his converts to repent for the forgiveness of their sins. He tells them to be crucified with Christ, to die to the world where the power of sin rules. As creatures of the new creation, they may sin. This happens when they act without full conviction, having doubts (Rom. 14:23). Faith requires certainty; it is not enough to have a predominant feeling. Paul pronounces a beatitude on those who do not act without faith: "Happy is he how has no reason to judge himself for what he approves" (Rom. 14:22). Within the new creation the law has no power to condemn. Sinners are condemned by what they approve and do while lacking conviction, without a "clear conscience," with a divided heart.

It happens, however, that most people prefer to have things spelled out for them in an objective way. What proceeds from faith is not something that can be observed clearly by others. After all, as Paul says, what counts is that the believer, after having carefully evaluated the situation, is fully convinced that she or he is doing God's will. If, on the other hand, sin is the transgression of the law, no evaluation is required. With the exception of "You shall not covet," the law only deals with sins that can be observed by others. Because of its lack of objectivity, Paul's understanding of sin in the lives of those who live crucified with Christ has not been widely accepted. He had to deal with those who insisted on dealing with sin on the basis of the law, both conservatives who found security in the law, and libertines who considered all things lawful since freedom from the law means that sin is no longer an issue.

In *To the Galatians* Paul argues against those who have another gospel, which he judges to be no gospel at all (Gal. 1:6). According to this gospel sin is the transgression of the law and righteousness is attained by observance of the law. This means that Christians still live under the law, and must perform works of law. Paul considers this gospel a perversion of the gospel of Christ (Gal. 1:7). The truth of the Gospel (Gal. 2:5) is that Christians are free from the law. They do not live under the law. One of the immediate corollaries to this is that they need not be circumcised (Gal. 2:3), which is the mark of those living under the law, and they may eat non-kosher with Gentiles (Gal. 2:12). When Paul had preached to them, they had accepted the Gospel and had enjoyed satisfaction with the reception of the Spirit and its power (Gal. 3:3 – 5, 4:15). Now some of them were about to follow the advice of another Christian missionary who wished to circumcise them and make them live under the law (Gal. 4:21). His argument was that they needed to be children of Abraham in order to be heirs of the promise God had given to Abraham. He pointed out that sons of Abraham are those who like Isaac are circumcised.

According to Paul, to follow the advice of this preacher would be a return to slavery to the law. More significantly, he tells those who wish to be circumcised: "You are severed from Christ, you who would be justified by the law" (Gal. 5:4). In other words, they would cease to be members of the body of the Risen Christ. One may recall in this context that to the Romans Paul wrote, "You have died to the law through the body of Christ" (Rom. 7:4). In the body of Christ the law is no longer effective.

To the Galatians, Paul points out that Abraham was justified on account of his faith, before he was circumcised (Gal. 3:6 – 9, 15 – 18). The heirs of Abraham are all those who live by faith on the promise God made to Abraham. They are sons of Abraham born of Sarah, the free woman. Those born according to the flesh through Hagar are not Abraham's heirs. Paul ends his argument saying, "So, brethren, we are not children of the slave but of the free woman" (Gal. 4:31). Paul asks the Galatians to consider the difference between "the works of the flesh" and "the fruit of the Spirit." (Gal. 5:19 – 24). The heirs of Abraham do have responsibilities. Paul writes: "Let us have no self-conceit, no provocation of one another, no envy of one another" (Gal. 5:26). This appeal is for a happy life in community. Then he considers an unhappy contingency, "Brethren, if a man is overtaken in any trespass, you who are spiritual should restore him in a spirit of gentleness. Look to yourself, lest you too be tempted. Bear one another's burdens and so fulfil the law of Christ" (Gal. 6:1 – 2). Apparently not all the Galatian Christians were "bewitched" (Gal. 3:1) by the apostle of circumcision. Paul appeals to those he designates as "spirituals" to remedy the situation brought about by the trespass of a fellow Christian. He does not tell them to condemn the sinner who committed the trespass, to deal with him according to the law that condemns him. He tells them, instead, to follow the law of Christ, which, rather than to define sins and condemn sinners, orders them to restore the sinner in the spirit of gentleness, bearing one another's burdens.

On the other hand, Paul has no patience with the one "who is troubling you." Paul is sure that he "will bear his judgment, whoever he is" (Gal. 5:10). It is easy to see that Paul would have felt quite certain that this apostle was not acting on the basis of faith. While he leaves this other apostle in the hands of his Judge, it is obvious that Paul does not wish him well. In fact, revealing the degree of his frustration with what is happening in the church at Galatia, he wishes that this preacher of circumcision, rather that to cut the foreskins of the Galatian Christians, would apply the knife to himself and accidentally cut the whole penis (Gal. 5:12). No doubt, Paul was a man with strong emotions, and when he wrote Galatians he was running out of patience with those who were constantly, in one way or another, trying to undo his work.

In *To the Corinthians I* and *II*, Paul has to deal with Christians who have taken the Gospel to the other extreme. While the one disturbing the Galatians told them that the cross, even if a significant demonstration of God's love, had not made any structural change to God's work of salvation on behalf of fallen humanity, the super-apostles who preached to the Corinthians told them that the cross had changed everything. They were already spiritual beings in need of nothing, and for them all things are lawful (1 Cor. 6:12; 10:23). They were already filled; they were rich (1 Cor. 4:8). Life in Christ meant full freedom from sin; therefore, the Corinthians felt they were already experiencing life beyond the reach of sin and the law. They were strong (1 Cor. 10:12), spiritual beings who could eat at pagan temples (1 Cor. 8:10; 10:21), and join themselves with prostitutes (1 Cor. 6:15 – 16). More specifically, Paul addresses them about a man who "is living with his father's wife," and charges them saying, "you are arrogant!" (1 Cor. 5:1 – 2). It would seem that thinking that they were beyond the power of sin, having already achieved full redemption, had made them libertines, rather than members of the body of Christ. It is noteworthy that to them Paul writes, "But I, brethren, could not address you as spiritual men, but as men of the flesh, as babes in Christ" (1 Cor. 3:1), quite the opposite of what he does when he writes to some Galatians and identifies them as "spirituals" who have rejected "the gospel of the circumcision,"

The way in which Paul wishes the Corinthians to deal with the man living with his father's wife is quite different from the way in which he deals with the one perturbing the Galatians. That Paul refers to the woman as the wife of the man's father rather than his mother would seem to indicate that his father is now married to someone other than his mother. That Paul views the situation as extremely grave is revealed by his comment that this is a case of immorality "of a kind that is not found even among pagans." That Paul charges the members of the church with arrogance would seem to indicate that they were saying to the culprit: "More power to you for pulling such a stunt." This demonstrates the consequences of thinking that one has escaped the power of sin. Those who think so sink even deeper into sin, no matter how it is defined. Paul wishes he could be at Corinth to deal with the situation, but apparently that was not possible right then. He issues a strict directive, instead: "Let him who has done this be removed from among you. For though absent in body I am present in spirit, and as if present, I have already pronounced judgment in the name of the Lord Jesus on the man who has done such a thing. When you are assembled, and my spirit is present, with the power of our Lord Jesus, you are to deliver this man to Satan for the destruction of the flesh, that his spirit may be saved in the day of the Lord Jesus" (1 Cor. 5:2 – 5).

In this case, Paul leaves no doubt that he takes sin seriously. He passes judgment and wishes the Corinthians to sever this man from the body of Christ, to deliver him to Satan. The last phrase is somewhat difficult to interpret with certainty. What does Paul mean by "deliver him to Satan for the destruction of the flesh that his spirit may be saved in the day of the Lord Jesus"? It would appear that he is saying that he will have to live in the world of Satan until he dies, that is outside the church. On what basis, then, is his spirit going to be saved at the Parousia? This is, indeed, a hard saying of Paul. It also stands at odds with his insistence that Christians should not judge each other, that they are all servants of Christ and only their Master has the right to judge their performance (Rom. 14:4). Clearly, he would have preferred not to have had to pass judgment in the name of the Lord Jesus. He points out, "If we judge ourselves truly, we should not be judged. But when we are judged by the Lord, we are chastened so that we may not be condemned along with the world" (1 Cor. 11:31 – 32). Apparently this is the context for his judgment in the name of the Lord of the man who lived with his father's wife. Such judgment is a chastening that prevents condemnation at the final judgment. The rationale for this remains obscure.

Paul certainly taught that the cross and the resurrection of Christ were the means by which God had brought about a cosmic turning of the ages. He did not think, however, that This Age had been replaced by The Age to Come. He understood that The Age of Messiah had come, and he was waiting for the Parousia and the Age to Come to arrive in the very near future. He fought valiantly against both those who denied that the cross and the resurrection had made a significant change and those who affirmed that it had changed everything. While for Christians sin is no longer the transgression of the law, it is still the case that Christians live in the flesh and in the Spirit. Sinning is a problem that needs to be taken seriously by those living between This Age and The Age to Come. Paul makes clear that at the Final Judgment sinners will face condemnation and eschatological death.

Paul's definition of sin as that which is not of faith is, in many ways, a good key to his theology. It is also one of the main reasons Paul has been misrepresented, ignored or misunderstood throughout the history of Christianity. The author of the *Second Letter of Peter* reports that Paul wrote some things that are "hard to understand, which the ignorant and unstable twist" (2 Pet. 3:15). In the twentieth century, one Pauline scholar is reputed to have said that through the centuries the only one who understood Paul was Marcion, a second century Roman Christian, and he misunderstood him. Marcion understood Paul by affirming that Christ had put an end to life under the law, but he misunderstood Paul when he thought that, therefore, the whole Old Testament should not be part of the Christian canon. Paul's definition of sin, as that which is not of faith rather than the transgression of the law, has not been accepted in traditional Christianity. Christianity has distinguished the Ten Commandments from the rest of the law and given them eternal validity as the definers of sin. The commonly made distinction between the moral and the ceremonial laws in the Old Testament, however, is one not made by any biblical author, much less Paul. As an institution, Christianity could not leave the definition of sin to the mind of Christians who are empowered and guided by the Spirit. Paul, of course, did not envision such development. He thought the *Parousia* would take place any day soon.

X. The Obedience of Faith

Paul saw the cross and the resurrection of Christ as the end of an era and the creation of a new humanity. The cross and the resurrection, as seen by faith, are acts of God. By one, God has broken the power of sin over humankind. By the other, God has created new life in the Spirit for the benefit of all human beings. In all this Jesus is viewed as an obedient agent who lived by his faith in God. He was, as Paul says, "born of woman, born under the law." His mission, however, was not to obey the law. It was "to redeem those who were under the law" (Gal. 4:4).

To do this, Jesus did not submit to the law's power and prove that it could be obeyed. His mission was to take away not only the power of sin, but also the power of the law. He was to make it possible for human beings not to have to live under the law. As Paul says, "we are not under law but under grace" (Rom. 6:15). Jesus' mission was not to demonstrate how to live a life without sin in the realm in which sinning and the law held sway, but to demonstrate how to live by faith.

Paul repeatedly refers to "the faith of Jesus" as something to be emulated. It is unfortunate that most translations of Paul render this phrase as "faith in Jesus." Paul's message is that Jesus himself lived by faith in God. His obedience was "the obedience of faith," which Paul is working to instill in his converts (Rom. 15:8). The life of faith is the life of the new creation by the power of the Spirit. Paul also refers to it as "the hearing of faith." In this connection it must be noted that in Hebrew the verb *shamah* means both to hear and to obey. The one who obeys is the one who has actually heard. Those who do not act on what they are told have not really *heard*.

The hearing of faith is what characterizes a Christian. Of course, this means that there must be those who preach the Gospel so that others may hear it (Rom. 10:14). Paul recognizes that, on the other hand, "Moses writes that the man who practices the righteousness which is based on the law shall live by it" (Rom. 10:5). The problem is that the people to whom the law had been given proved to be "disobedient and contrary" (Rom. 10:21, quoting Is. 65:2), and they all failed to obey it. Israel did try to obtain the righteousness which is based on the law, but "did not succeed in fulfilling that law. Why? Because they did not pursue it through faith, but as if it were based on works" (Rom. 9:31 – 32). For Paul, even in the times of historical Israel, the pursuit of righteousness was to be through faith, as Abraham, the founding patriarch, exemplified. Paul explains the pursuit of righteousness through faith by quoting the Scriptures, "The righteousness based on faith says, Do not say in your heart, 'Who will ascend into heaven?' (that is, to bring Christ down) or 'Who will descend into the abyss?' (that is, to bring Christ up from the dead). But what does it say? The word is near you on your lips and in your heart (that is, the word of faith which we preach); . . . For man believes with his heart and so is justified, and he confesses with his lips and so is saved" (Rom. 10:6 – 9). The righteousness of faith does not demand outlandish performances.

The righteousness that is based on faith is one in which the faith that is lodged in the heart finds expression through the body that confesses by its actions. In other words, it seeks the integration of the person. It is characterized by the correspondence between actions and convictions, and results in the obedience of faith (Rom. 1:5; 16:26). Of course, not all those to whom the Gospel is preached hear and obey (Rom. 10:16), but those who actually hear the Gospel obey it (1 Cor. 9:13). What must be recognized is that while Paul does not connect salvation to the law, he does connect salvation to obedience. Faith in God's action at the cross and the resurrection of Christ does include a way of being in the world that is activated and guided by the Spirit that raised Christ from the dead. The obedience of faith is the conduct of those guided by the Spirit. The obedience of faith is not related to the definition of sin found in the law. Those who fail to live out the obedience of faith fail on the basis of Paul's definition of sin as "that which is not of faith" (Rom. 14:23). This definition of sin is the one that informs the obedience of faith. The obedience of faith is not obedience to the law.

The grace of God brought about new life by having the Spirit pour out God's love into the hearts of women and men. God's grace justifies those who believe with their hearts and saves those who confess the power of the Gospel by their way of being. Grace does not work through the law. It operates "apart from works of law" (Rom. 4:6), "apart from the law" (Rom. 3:21). Thus, it is impossible for any human being to take credit for his or her good standing before God. Paul, therefore, regards "boasting" a particularly offensive activity. If "works of law" are the means of salvation, boasting would not only be allowable but valid. As Paul says, "If Abraham was justified by works, he has something to boast about." The statement offers a contrary to fact condition. Then he asks, "What does the Scripture say? 'Abraham believed God, and it was reckoned to him as righteousness.'" Paul leaves no doubt that Abraham could not have boasted before God because he had been considered righteous by God without having done anything (Rom. 4:2 – 3). Then he asks rhetorically, Were his descendent blessed on account of their works? Not at all, he answers. It was before the children of Isaac and Rebecca were born, before they could have done anything that God chose the younger as the heir and told Rebecca, "The elder will serve the younger." Thus the line of descendants of Abraham according to the promise was not established "because of works but because of his [God's] call" (Rom. 9:11 – 12). As far as Paul is concerned, salvation has always been dependent on God's initiative alone, that is, on grace. It is God who calls, who loves, who justifies. It was so with Abraham and the patriarchs, and it is so to this day.

Abraham was justified by God on account of his faith and, Paul insists, so it is even now for both Jews and Gentiles. When Paul refers to faith, however, it must be noticed that he does not have in mind mental agreement to a proposition, as is the case, for example, in the *Letter of James*. According to its author, if one says, "God is one," anyone who agrees with the statement may be called a believer. But, as the author also says, when faith is understood as belief, then "even the demons believe and shudder" (Jas. 2:19). When conceived this way it is proper to think that faith is not enough as a mark of discipleship. Works, such as "to visit orphans and widows in their affliction, and to keep oneself unstained by the world" (Jas. 1:27) must supplement belief so that religion may have a foundation and relevance in human experience. Given the examples used by the author of the *Letter of James*, it would appear that he wrote to argue against a misinterpretation of Paul, and there is abundant evidence that there were many such misinterpretations around at the time (2 Pet. 3:15 – 16). In this case, it would appear, the misunderstanding is in the way Paul refers to faith. For him, faith is a way of being in the world that joined with hope manifests itself as a love that obeys the guidance of the Holy Spirit. It is not agreement to a proposition that is considered intellectually sound. It is acting according to the full convictions of one's renewed mind.

Both Paul and James quote the text from Genesis which says that "Abraham believed God and it was reckoned to him as righteousness" (Rom 4:3; Jas. 2:23). But Paul does not give to the text the context given to it by the author of the *Letter of James,* in which Abraham demonstrated his faith by his willingness to sacrifice his son Isaac (Jas. 2:21). For Paul, Abraham demonstrated his faith when he believed God's promise (Rom. 4:13), before Isaac was born, before either of them was circumcised (Rom. 4:10). For Paul, faith cannot be a virtue, a work (Rom. 4:2f.). If faith "works," it is not to establish a person's claim on salvation. If it works at all, it is because God's promise is being fulfilled. The work of faith does not have as its object to satisfy the requirements of the law or to gain ground before God. Rather, faith works because of the integration of the person by the power of the Spirit that has poured God's love into the hearts of those who have faith in God.

Paul expects faith to work, but insisting on the fulfillment of works of law is a denial of the resurrection of Christ as a new creation. To point this out, he writes, "For in Christ Jesus neither circumcision nor uncircumcision is of any avail, but faith working through love" (Gal. 5:6). The life of faith makes effective God's love by what it accomplishes for the benefit of society. Paul, as noticed in a previous meditation, encourages everyone to use his reasoning powers to the fullest so that "each one [may] test his own work" (Gal. 6:4). Writing to the Corinthians about contributing to the "collection" of money he intends to take to Jerusalem for the relief of the poor Christians in that city, he assures them that "God is able to provide you with every blessing in abundance, so that you may always have enough of everything and may provide in abundance for every good work" (2 Cor. 9:8). In *To the Corinthians I* he points out that he has established the only possible foundation, Jesus Christ, on which every Christian must build a life. What each one builds, however, will be tested by fire. "If the work which any man has built on the foundation survives, he will receive a reward" (1 Cor. 3:14). Undoubtedly, Paul thought that the life of faith is a work, but it is not a "work of law." It is a work of love guided by the Spirit, an obedience of faith. This is dependent on Paul's definition of sin. While in the world of Adam sin is the transgression of the law, in the world of the Risen Christ "Whatever does not proceed from faith is sin" (Rom. 14:23).

What the author of the *Letter of James* calls "work" when he argues that "faith apart from works is dead" (Jas. 2:26), Paul designates as the "fruit of the Spirit." The fruit of the Spirit manifests itself in all the different aspects of the life of those who have faith in God. The tree of the Spirit gives abundant fruit, but even though it is all the produce of the one source it is not all the same. The fruit has the same beneficial effect, but it adapts itself to circumstantial needs. Paul describes it as "love, joy, peace, patience, kindness, goodness, faithfulness, gentleness, self-control; against such there is no law" (Gal. 5:22 – 23). The "works" produced by this fruit are natural activities of all those who "have crucified the flesh with its passions and desires" and now live by the power of the Risen Christ as "those who belong to Christ Jesus" (Gal. 5:24).

It is in this context that Paul gives his ultimate ethical instruction concerning the obedience of faith. He uses a most telling structure for its presentation. The commandment given in the imperative mode is dependent on a description of the situation in the indicative mode. The statement is a true to fact conditional sentence: "If we live by the Spirit, let us also walk by the Spirit" (Gal. 5:25). Faith is a way of being, a way of living, living in the dispensation and by the power of the Spirit. Christians who have joined Christ in his crucifixion of the flesh and his resurrection by the power of the Spirit, and who are endowed with the fruit of the Spirit must "walk." This is the colloquial way of saying "conduct life," "work," "influence others," "live." The obedience of faith is "walking by the Spirit." True to his vision that the mind renewed by the Spirit is capable of discerning the will of God, Paul does not elaborate a set of rules, a new law, for those who walk by the Spirit. The obedience of faith is obedience to the convictions of the mind renewed by the Spirit. God pours love freely into the hearts of those who believe so that they may perform their faith. Paul's commandment is "Pursue love" (1 Cor. 14:1). The standard for the Christian life is set by the power for life that emanates from the Risen Christ and enables those who are in Christ to be guided according to the will of God.

For Paul, faith does not have to do with the intellectual grasping of God's activity. Christian faith is the "obedience of faith" (Rom. 1:5; 15:18; 16:26). The demands of faith are beyond rationalizations because they are imposed by the Holy Spirit. Christian obedience is not to an objectified standard, to commandments that can be rationalized. It is obedience to a subjective power that renews the mind and transforms the heart when the Spirit pours God's love. Christians live by faith when they live manifesting their faith in acts that objectify the love that energizes their being.

As Paul says, Christians are controlled by the love of Christ (2 Cor. 5:14). It is not their love for God, but the love of God that the Holy Spirit has poured into their hearts that controls them. They do not live controlled by the law mediated through Moses and angels (Gal. 3:19), but by the love of God poured into their hearts by the Spirit. The love that controls them fulfills the law of God (Rom. 13:8), the law to which Paul's mind agrees (Rom. 7:22). The obedience of faith is manifested in lives that express the faith and the hope that is energized by the love of God that brought about a new creation by raising Christ from the dead. True Christian obedience is powered from within by a mind renewed by the Spirit.

XI. THE LIFE I NOW LIVE IN THE FLESH

I have pointed out in previous meditations that Paul's apocalypticism is not characterized by descriptions of battles between superhuman adversaries and details of how specific evils are to be punished before human history comes to a horrific conclusion. Paul rejects the apocalyptic obsession with the future and grounds Christian life on the manifestation of God's righteousness in God's past actions at the cross and the resurrection; these events are at the center of Paul's understanding of the righteousness of God. Still, he affirms the approaching *Parousia*, the appearance of Christ in glory, as a certainty which is worthy of fervent Christian hope. Christians are now living in a fallen world, but their hope for the future, sustained by their faith in what God has already done in the past, gives them salvation as they partake of the creation of the Risen Christ. Fervent apocalyptic expectations may cause disengagement from what is happening in the world. For Paul, however, faith and hope in Christ are not a way of escaping from the troubles, the sufferings, the vicissitudes and the joys of earthly life. They require serious involvement in the life being lived in the present evil age.

It is not uncommon for Christians to wish to escape from the responsibilities and the struggles of life in society. Thus, at times, Christians have sought to become "otherworldly" by withdrawing from society into monastic orders, counter-cultural sectarianism, individualistic narcissism, etc. Even if the gospel *According to John* is most often the foundation on which the justification of such conduct is based, the letters of Paul have also been marshalled as evidence. Many Christians have read Paul as one who espouses withdrawal from the world into an ascetic lifestyle.

The gospel *According to John* frequently refers to "the world" as a place where both Jesus and his disciples after him find rejection, persecution and death. Paul has a different vocabulary. He refers to life in "the flesh." Just as in the gospel *According to John* "the world" may refer to quite different and contrasting conditions of life and classes of people, so also "the flesh" is used by Paul to cover a broad spectrum of meanings as he uses it with different Greek prepositions. In particular, we shall see how he distinguishes "in (*en*) the flesh" from "according to (*kata*) the flesh," the antithesis of "according to (*kata*) the Spirit." Exploring the richness of his phraseology is a rewarding path to his theology.

In Paul's lexicon, the word "flesh" does not necessarily refer to the material found in the bodies of humans and other animals. Paul comes closest to this meaning when he argues that the body humans now have is not to be the body which they will have at the resurrection of the dead. He points out that "not all flesh is alike, but there is one kind for men, another for animals, another for birds, and another for fish" (1 Cor. 15:39). The point is that different bodies have different "flesh," and therefore different "glories." Thus, he continues, "There are celestial bodies and there are terrestrial bodies, but the glory of the celestial is one and the glory of the terrestrial is another" (1 Cor. 15:40). Among the terrestrial bodies, the flesh of humans, other animals, birds and fish are different because these beings live in different environments, or ecological systems. His biology, it would seem, is limited to a classification according to land, air and water, somewhat corresponding to the story of creation where on the first three days God creates three environments and in the next three he creates the life forms corresponding to each. Paul's observation about the different flesh in the animal kingdom tells us that he is giving the word "flesh" a special meaning.

This seems to be confirmed by the way Paul's argument comes to a close. His agenda is to show that the resurrection life is going to be lived in a spiritual body which belongs to a totally different order of "glory" from the one humans have in bodies of flesh. He states his conclusion with a surprising twist. Having established that there are differences among bodies with different flesh, he writes, "So it is with the resurrection of the dead. What is sown is perishable, what is raised is imperishable. It is sown in dishonor, it is raised in glory. It is sown in weakness, it is raised in power. It is sown a physical body, it is raised a spiritual body" (1 Cor. 15:42 – 44). What is surprising is that the body that is "sown," that is, buried, is not a "fleshly," or a "physical" body. The Greek does not read *sarkikon*, or *physikon*. It reads, *psyxikon*, belonging to a soul. Paul gives the rationale for it by quoting the Genesis story: "The first man, Adam, became a living soul [*psyxen zosan*]" (1 Cor. 15:45). Human life in the creation of Adam is "soul" [*psyxikon*] life. Humans do not *have* souls. They *are* souls that, since the Fall, are flesh. Humans now live in an environment that is not the same as the one in which Adam, the first man, was created. It is most revealing, therefore, that Paul reverts to the description of the creation of the first man in Genesis 2:7 when he wishes to contrast human life now with the life of those who experience resurrection from the dead. This makes the point that the resurrection is not a return to the pre-fallen condition of Adam, but a transformation to a much superior spiritual body. As he says, what is sown is perishable, that is, mortal. Adam was not created immortal as a living soul. He needed to have access to the tree of life in order to live. By contrast, the life in a spirit body of those who will be raised at the return of Christ is going to be life that is imperishable and eternal. For Paul, the future is the realization of the fullness of life in the Spirit, not a return to the Garden of Eden.

That humans live in bodies of flesh would seem obvious, but for Paul it is important to emphasize this fact. At times he uses one of the words "body" or "flesh" to refer to the other, and translators have, therefore, translated the Greek *sarx* (=flesh) as "body." For example, the RSV reads, "Since we have these promises, beloved, let us cleanse ourselves from every defilement of body [*sarx*] and spirit" (2 Cor. 7:1). Of course, throughout Paul's letters Christians are understood to live both in the flesh and in the Spirit. A few verses down, Paul says that he had been anxious about the Corinthians and had started to travel toward them. Having crossed from Asia Minor to Macedonia, he says, "our bodies had no rest but we were afflicted at every turn — fighting without and fear within. But God, who comforts the downcast, comforted us by the coming of Titus" with good news about the Corinthians (2 Cor. 7:5 – 6). Paul, however, wrote "our flesh had no rest." Since the good news brought by Titus was sufficient to ameliorate the condition of his *flesh*, we may safely infer that in Macedonia he was not suffering from some bodily ailment. His affliction in the *flesh* was in fact psychological (*psyxikon*).

The same, most likely, is also the case in Paul's reference to his "thorn in the flesh," which he describes further as "a messenger from Satan to harass me, to keep me from being too elated" (2 Cor. 12:7). There has been quite a bit of speculation about Paul's thorn in the flesh. Since he apologizes to the Galatians about signing his letter with unseemly large letters (Gal. 6:11), it has been suggested that Paul must have suffered from poor eyesight, and could not write small letters which he could not see. Those offering this explanation point out also that Paul was suffering from a bodily ailment while in Galatia and credited his hosts for their willingness to give him their eyes (Gal. 4:13, 15). It seems more likely to me that the thorn in the flesh was not at all a physical condition, but an emotional or mental one, an affliction of the soul, or of the heart. To be noticed also is that when he tells the Galatians that he is tired of the false charges other apostles make against him, charges which cause his converts to be perturbed (Gal. 1:7), Paul reminds them, "Henceforth let no man trouble me; for I bear on my body the marks of Jesus" (Gal. 6:17). In this case he is surely referring to the marks on his body from the many beatings he had received from his torturers. In this way he saw himself participating in the passion of Christ. In any case, he certainly knew the difference between afflictions of the soul and afflictions of the body, but the words he uses to identify them sometimes are less than clear. Most often Paul refers to the flesh to indicate a condition of being, not necessarily the body's physical material.

Translators also have seen Paul's use of the word "flesh" as a reference to the world. Thus, the judgment that those who marry will experience "troubles of the flesh" (1 Cor. 7:28) is rendered as "worldly troubles" (RSV). These are not troubles that affect the body, but the troubles that accompany the demands of life in the world. The point becomes clear when Paul defends his conduct and that of his associates Silvanus and Timothy. Having just told the Corinthians that he planned to visit them before going to Judea, he asks rhetorically, "Was I vacillating when I wanted to do this?" In other words, had he been sincere when he said that he had planned on visiting them? Or was he saying it when he had no intention of doing so? He reframes the question, "Do I make my plans like a worldly man, ready to say Yes and No at once?" (2 Cor. 1:17). The Greek reads, "The things I plan, do I plan them according to the flesh?" In this case "according to the flesh" has been translated "like a worldly man."

The conduct of life in the world makes demands that are troublesome and questionable. Double talk is not uncommon. Do the Corinthians think Paul is acting as is normal in society? Paul also says this from the opposite perspective. "For though we live in the world we are not carrying on a worldly war" (2 Cor. 10:3). The Greek reads, "For though we walk in the flesh, we are not fighting according to the flesh." The distinction he makes here is crucial for him. To live "in" the flesh, in the world, in nature, in history is not an option; to conduct one's life "according to" the flesh, according to what is normal among humans in nature and history is sinful. As Paul says, "if you live according to the flesh you will die" (Rom. 8:13).

Paul finds himself repeatedly defending his mission. Thus, he writes, "Our boast is this, the testimony of our conscience that we have behaved in the world, and still more toward you, with holiness and godly sincerity, not by earthly wisdom but by the grace of God" (2 Cor. 1:12). It is important for him to establish that he does not behave according to what the Greek original characterizes as "fleshly [*sarkike*] wisdom." For Paul, the "flesh" is the natural environment where humans live according to standards of conduct that are under the power of sin and death. The word describes the human condition in a fallen world.

Paul refers to human life now as "life in the flesh." As a Christian who through baptism has participated in the death and the resurrection of Christ (Rom 6:6 – 11) and is, therefore, a new creation (2 Cor. 5:17), Paul recognizes that he still lives "in the flesh." He confesses in a most emphatic way, "*ego de sarkinos eimi,*" "but I am myself fleshly" (Rom. 7:14). Writing to the Romans about the difference between being a slave to sin and a slave to righteousness, Paul recognizes that this is no easy matter, and explains himself saying, "I am speaking in human terms, because of your natural limitations" (Rom. 6:19). Literally he wrote, "I speak as a man on account of the weakness of your flesh."

All humans live "in the weakness of the flesh," with natural limitations. Weakness is the main characteristic of the realm of the flesh. Even the law once it entered the human world was "weakened by the flesh," and therefore it could not prevent sin. It could only define, or reveal sin (Rom. 8:3). Because of the weakness of the flesh, all who live in the flesh sin. It is instructive to note that while Paul understands that the law was weakened by the flesh, so that it became "the law of sin," he does not say that God sent his Son to the realm of the flesh where sin reigns. He qualifies the incarnation saying that "God has done what the law could not do . . . sending his Son in the likeness of sinful flesh" (Rom. 8:3). Just as to say that man was made "after the likeness" of God (Gen. 1:26) is not saying that he was made a god, so to say that the Son was sent "in the likeness of sinful flesh" is not saying that he was made flesh. In this Paul differs from the gospel *According to John* (Jn. 1:14).

The human condition under the power of sin is described by Paul as life in the flesh. He qualifies this condition by recognizing that Christians, who on account of their baptism live "in Christ" and "in the flesh," are no longer under the power of sin. While admitting that he has no choice but to live in the flesh, in nature, however, Paul at times says that Christians no longer live in the flesh. It would seem that by this he means that they are not under the power of sin. He says, for example, that "those who are in the flesh cannot please God" (Rom. 8:8). Then he tells the Romans, "But you are not in the flesh" (Rom. 8:9). Speaking of the past he writes, "while we were living in the flesh, our sinful passions, aroused by the law, were at work in our members to bear fruit for death" (Rom. 7:5). These passages give the impression that Christians are no longer living in the flesh. Paul, however, is quite aware that this is not quite the case, as noticed above. It would seem that he actually means that while still living "in" the flesh, Christians do not live under the power of sin "according to" the flesh, and are not under the law that condemns sinners to death.

In a more revealing and very affirming passage he says, "the life I now live in the flesh I live by faith in the Son of God, who loved me and gave himself for me" (Gal. 2:20). Living in the flesh by faith is living "according to" the Spirit, is living "crucified with Christ." That is the predicament of Christians in the present evil age. They live in the flesh and in Christ. Paul also expresses this tension from another perspective. Living in the flesh, one walks by sight, on the basis of natural endowments. Paul reminds his readers, however, "We walk by faith, not by sight" (1 Cor. 5:7). Walking by faith is living according to the Spirit in the new creation.

Christians do not escape from the realities of the present. They are, however, free from the power of the law, sin and eschatological death, while still living in the flesh. They are crucified with Christ and, like Christ while on earth, they experience the tensions of being unable to accommodate themselves to the norms that seem natural in the fallen world. Paul puts it plainly: "The desires of the flesh are against the Spirit, and the desires of the Spirit are against the flesh; for these are opposed to each other to prevent you from doing what you would . . . . Those who belong to Christ Jesus have crucified the flesh with its passions and desires" (Gal. 5:17, 24).

But even when the passions and the desires of the flesh have been crucified with Christ, and have been left buried with Christ in the waters of baptism, Christians still live in the flesh. This reality is one Paul cannot deny, even if at times he says that Christians no longer live "in the flesh" (Rom. 7:5).

The desires of the flesh which those who live in Christ have crucified, it must be noted, are not just those which are usually called "carnal" passions. They include jealousy, envy, strife, gossip, hypocrisy, blasphemy, etc. These are not at all things that can in any way be attached to the biological instincts in human beings. The "sinful passions," that as Paul says, are "aroused by the law" (Rom. 7:5) are not necessarily carnal, sexual passions, but very much sins that dwell in the soul, in the character of a person. Paul then lists the things exhibited by those who are led by the Spirit, "love, joy, peace, patience, kindness, goodness, faithfulness, gentleness, self-control" (Gal. 5:22). These are not otherworldly ideals, but very much the stuff of a well lived life in the flesh.

Paul also personifies the "flesh" as an entity that functions among the other agents that populate his symbolic universe. As was already noticed, he says that the flesh weakens the law so that it cannot do what it was supposed to do. He advises his converts to "make no provisions for the flesh, to gratify its desires" (Rom. 13:14), and to "not use your freedom as an opportunity for the flesh" (Gal. 5:13). It would be quite wrong to think that Paul has particularly in mind sexual impulses, as is most often understood today. That the flesh is anxious to find opportunities to satisfy itself, but needs provisions in order to do that only tells us that the flesh functions as a whole person. Does the flesh have a mind of its own that makes it able to take advantage of opportunities? Apparently the flesh makes claims that cause people to feel that they owe it provisions for its satisfaction. Paul personifies the flesh as an actor to be taken into account.

According to Paul, those who belong to Christ have crucified the flesh (Gal. 5:24). Along this line, Paul writes, "So then, brethren, we are debtors, not to the flesh, to live according to the flesh"

(Rom 8:12). Of course, we are debtors to God who gives life to those who live in Christ. Paul, however, feels the need to make clear that we are not debtors to the flesh. He elaborates on the consequences of providing for, giving opportunities to, or paying debts to the flesh rather than crucifying it. "For he who sows to his own flesh will from the flesh reap corruption." Again, this must be understood in Pauline terms, that is, as a reference to the whole of life and not particularly to carnal or sexual desires. By contrast, "he who sows to the Spirit will from the Spirit reap eternal life" (Gal. 6:8). Those who sow to the Spirit, of course, have crucified the flesh, that is, they no longer live the natural life of the human environment that has fallen under the power of the "elemental spirits of the world." They actualize the obedience of faith.

The personification of the flesh in all these texts allows us to see the mental world of the apostle as one in which the world is full of powerful agents which must be taken to account in order to live fruitful lives. While affirming the reality of salvation by the power of the Spirit that raised Christ from the dead, Paul is constantly aware of the life he is now living in the mortal body of flesh. Living by faith, and not by sight, does not mean renouncing the responsibilities of life. Being a Christian in the present evil age is not easy precisely because living in the flesh, but according to the Spirit means that the Christian's life is not guided by the norms of "the flesh." This makes for inner tensions in the lives of Christians. The Christian life, however, is rewarding because not living according to the flesh, that is, according to what is normally accepted, Christians enjoy freedom to express their faith and hope in acts of love according to the Spirit.

XII  Glorify God in Your Body

As noted in my previous meditation, Paul seems at times to use the words *flesh* and *body* interchangeably. This may have been due to biblical Hebrew's lack of words for abstract concepts, such as *body*. When reading the Old Testament in English, whenever one reads "body" the Hebrew original may be flesh, belly, back, bone, thigh, carcass or soul. Paul uses the expression "mortal flesh" and "mortal body," or "sinful flesh" and "sinful body" with no apparent difference in meaning. When he speaks of flesh or body as being in the world, they are characterized as being sinful and mortal. As pointed out in a previous meditation, humans may live "in the flesh" or they may live "in the Spirit," that is "in Christ." The "flesh" thus refers to the natural ecological system of the fallen creation in which human life is normally lived. Since the flesh is also characteristically weak, sin and death reign in this environment. As long as human beings live in the "soul bodies" in which Adam came to life they have no option but to live in the flesh.

Hebrew thought, as part of the way of thinking in the ancient Near East, was tied to the material basis of existence. As already noted, the Hebrew language lacked a word for the body. The body is more than just the sum of its parts. In order for the members to be a body they must be organically joined together so that they are all nourished and able to grow together (Col. 2:18). Paul's usage of the word body builds on the abstract quality of the concept. He uses the word in reference to four kinds of human existence: being disembodied, "naked"; living in the body of sin, in the flesh; living in the body of Christ, in the Spirit, and living in the glorious, spiritual, resurrection body.

Life without a body could not be an active life, capable of expressing itself meaningfully and accomplishing things in relationship with others. A disembodied life, even if capable of being conceived, is not at all attractive. He is aware that in his trip to the third heaven he was not conscious of his body (2 Cor. 12:2), but his hopes for the future are not to experience "naked" existence (2 Cor. 5:3). His desire is to be clothed with the glorious resurrection body (2 Cor. 5:4). The disembodied existence of the dead in Christ who wait for the *Parousia* is no active life but like a sleep, a dormant state of waiting for the resurrection. When in prison at Rome, Paul recognizes that his prison term may end with his execution. He refers to it as a departure "to be with the Lord" (Phil. 1:23), but he is hard pressed to decide whether to desire it. The advantages of being with the Lord are neutralized by the realization that in his "nakedness" he would not be able to do what he does when in a body, namely, honor Christ (Phil. 1:20). When he writes that he wishes that "now as always Christ will be honored in my body whether by life or by death," he is saying that he hopes to honor Christ either by "fruitful labor" if he is released from prison, or by the manner in which he conducts himself at his execution should he be sentenced to death. He is aware of the need to die "nobly."

A human life that expresses itself in an accountable way can only be lived in a body (2 Cor. 5:10). The body is what objectifies a life and allows for relationships with others. The body is the means for living in the world. People who live in the world of Adam after the Fall, live in what Paul calls the body of sin (Rom 6:6). Living in the world of the Risen Christ, people live in the body of Christ (Rom. 7:4). Like the flesh, the body is also a way for Paul to describe the tension of Christian existence. The tension results from the incorporation of the believer into the body of Christ while still living in a mortal body (Rom. 6:12). This is the tension which, after he has analyzed it, causes Paul to dramatically cry, "Who will deliver me from this body of death" (Rom. 7:24). As a Christian,

Paul does not consider a disembodied life attractive. Neither does he consider it desirable to live in the body of sin, the body of life in the flesh. His preference is for the life made available in the body of Christ. Of course, the ultimate option is for life in the glorious spiritual body to be received at the resurrection from the dead.

While waiting for the *Parousia* and the reception of the immortal spiritual body, Christians are not condemned to live controlled by the limitations and the weaknesses of the body of sin. Their baptism has opened for them a new way of being. It is not yet life in the "spirit-body." It is life in the body of Christ (1 Cor. 12:13). Living in the fallen world, life in the spirit-body is not an option, but life in the body of Christ most certainly is. Christians who have died with Christ in the waters of baptism have put to death the "old man" who lived in the body of sin. They are, therefore, no longer servants of sin (Rom. 6:2). A Christian is a "new person" who serves God rather than sin and the law (Rom. 7:4). Still, Paul recognizes that while living as members of the body of Christ, Christians live in a body where the natural tendencies of the flesh are in operation, making their participation in the body of Christ somehow precarious. As a result, together with all creation, Christians also moan and groan while living in the world waiting for "the redemption of the body" that is subject to decay and death (Rom. 8:12f.).

Life in the body of Christ is life in the Spirit and by the power of the Spirit. Bodies are what objectify life, but life may be lived in different ecological systems. The body of sin lives in the flesh and according to the flesh. Members of the body of Christ live in the flesh and according to the Spirit. They have put to death the deeds of the body of sin, so as not to live according to the flesh. As members of the body of Christ they live to manifest the Risen Christ in the world (Rom. 12:4 f.; 1 Cor. 12:15 – 18). They glorify God in their bodies by making God's power and love effectively active in the world (1 Cor. 6:20).

Confronted by the report that the Corinthians were attending pagan temples and while there eating food that had been sacrificed to a pagan god, Paul builds an argument that is based on the notion that Christians as members of the body of Christ are no longer under the law. As discussed in *To the Corinthians I*, the question of whether or not to eat food that had been offered to an idol could arise under different circumstances. The Corinthian Christians considered themselves "spirituals" living above the mundane existence of sinful mortals. Their slogan proclaimed, "all things are lawful for me" (1 Cor. 6:12). According to them, Christians are free to eat what has been offered to an idol under any circumstance. In his consideration of the issue, Paul looks at three different scenarios.

The first is a rather simple one. A Christian who needs to provide food for his family asks himself, "May I go to buy meat at the butcher shop that sells the meat of the animals that have been sacrificed at Apollo's or Diana's temple?" Considering whether the meat sold at the butcher shop connected to a pagan temple may be eaten at a Christian home, Paul gives a very forthright ruling: "Eat whatever is sold in the meat market without raising any question on the ground of conscience." He supports his instruction with a Scriptural quotation: "For the earth is the Lord's and everything in it" (1 Cor. 10:25f.). That is, the animals whose meet is being eaten are provided by the Lord, and what was done with them at a temple did not change that in the least.

The second scenario is that of the Christian who has received a dinner invitation from a non-Christian friend. Paul thinks that if the Christian is disposed to accept the invitation, he can go to his friend's home and eat whatever his friend is serving for dinner (1 Cor. 10:27). This piece of advice would cause his fellow Jews to consider Paul an apostate Jew. Precisely because Jews wish to avoid finding themselves in a situation which would compromise the observance of kosher rules they would unquestionably reject such invitations. That is one of the main factors isolating them from their Gentile neighbors. Paul is a Jew who has become a new person in Christ and, therefore, no longer lives "under the law." As he says, "the kingdom of God does not mean food and drink" (Rom. 14:17). As concerns food and drink, Christians at home or at the home of a non-Christian friend could eat whatever is being graciously offered them with a clear conscience. For Paul food and drink are what the Stoics called "indifferent" (*adiaphora*). "Food will not commend us to God, we are no worse off if we do not eat, and no better off if we do" (1 Cor. 8:8). Paul would actually agree with the Corinthian "spirituals" who claimed to know that idols are nothing and, therefore, could not affect food one way or another.

This scenario, however, could be significantly modified if the inviting friend were to inform the Christian that the food being served had been offered to an idol at the household's private shrine. This information does not affect the food in any way. Neither does it affect the conscience of the Christian who is quite aware that idols are nothing and that food has no connection to the kingdom of God. What changes the situation is that the non-Christian friend has doubts about the propriety of a Christian eating food that has been offered to an idol. What the Christian has to consider now is the reason for having accepted the invitation to dine with his friend. He needs to determine how his ability to make God's love effective is going to be affected if his friend thinks he is a bad Christian who eats food offered to a pagan idol (1 Cor. 9:19 – 23; 14:28 – 33). The ethic of the kingdom of God is not an ethic of laws, but an ethic of love. What Christians must consider is their effectiveness as agents of the love of God. If that is the case, Paul would not eat the food out of love for a friend who has an immature understanding of the power of idols.

The third scenario considered by Paul is one in which the food is being eaten neither in a Christians's home nor at the home of a non-Christian friend. In this case Christians who consider themselves strong and who brag that "all things are lawful for me" are eating "at table in an idol's temple" (1 Cor. 8:10). Can a Christian have a meal at the idol's temple? Most likely the occasion is celebrating one of the idol's festivals. The rationale for this conduct may be easily imagined. Festivals are community affairs where neighbors enjoy each other's company. The food is good and the idol is a powerless piece of wood, marble or plaster. "Spirituals" feel free from the power of the principalities and powers of the world. Moreover, if Jewish Christians can celebrate Passover, Tabernacles and Dedication, there is no reason why Gentile Christians cannot celebrate their traditional feasts.

Considering this scenario, Paul offers strong objections to the notion that Christians are free to sit at table in an idol's temple. In the first place, according to his apocalyptic scenario, the gods and lords of the world are real (1 Cor. 8:5). They are present and rule over the proceedings at such feasts. Therefore, to eat at one of these temples is to eat at the table of demons. Idols are nothing, but gods and demons are a different matter (1 Cor. 10:19 f.). Moreover, such festivals are an integral part of a system of idolatry (1 Cor. 10:14) and immorality (1 Cor. 10:8). This means that while eating food may be an "indifferent" activity, being partners with demons cancels one's participation in the body of Christ (1 Cor. 10:20).

Eating at a table establishes communion, and members of the body of Christ should not have communion with demons. The freedom of the Christian is not freedom for living dangerously. "Let any one who thinks that he stands take heed less he fall" (1 Cor. 10:12). Paul reminds the Corinthians, who feel strong and knowledgeable, of the experience of the Israelites in the desert. Many of those who ate manna and drank from the rock that gave them miraculous water ended up dead in the desert at the hand of the destroyer because of their idolatry, their immorality and their dissatisfaction with what God provided for them (1 Cor. 10:1 – 11). Many who pass for members of the body of Christ, Paul warns, may be "guilty of profaning the body and the blood of the Lord" by thinking it possible to eat at the table of the Lord and at the table of demons (1 Cor. 10:21). A Christian cannot partake of "two breads" (1 Cor. 10:21f.) To the Christians who feel strong enough to stand by themselves and eat bread at both tables, Paul asks, "Shall we provoke the Lord to jealousy? Are you stronger than he?" (1 Cor. 10:22).

The context in which Paul brings to the fore the celebration of the Lord's Supper is a bit confusing. If, as most scholars believe, verses 2 – 16 of chapter 11 of *To the Corinthians I* are an interpolation by an editor of the letter, then Paul is commending the Corinthians because they "maintain the traditions even as I have delivered them to you" (1 Cor. 11:1). In the original, the following sentence establishes an exemption, "on the following instructions I do not commend you, because when you come together it is not for the better but for the worse" (1 Cor. 11:17). He then gives examples. The second is, "when you meet together, it is not the Lord's Supper that you eat" (1 Cor. 11:20). After describing what is actually happening at their common meals, Paul reports the tradition of the Last Supper (1 Cor. 11:23 – 26). This is in fact the earliest record of the Lord's Supper. Paul says he knows about it from the oral tradition. He places it in time and cites the words of Jesus instituting the bread and the wine as his body and his blood. The synoptic gospels also give almost exactly the same words. What is different about their reports is the accompanying explanation, which may have been part of the oral tradition or may have been provided by the authors of the gospels. Paul emphasizes that Jesus told them to eat and drink often. By doing it they were proclaiming the Lord's death until he comes (1 Cor. 11:26). *According to Mark* and *According to Matthew* have Jesus lament that he will not drink the fruit of the vine "until the day when I drink it new in the kingdom of God" (Mk. 14:25; Mt. 26:29). *According to Luke* has Jesus comment that he had been eager to celebrate Passover with his disciples, and lament that he will not eat it again "until it is fulfilled in the kingdom of God" (Lk. 22:15 – 16). *According to John* reports a meal but ignores the institution of the bread and the wine. Instead, Jesus washes the feet of the disciples and tells them to follow his example by washing each other's feet. All the gospels say that at the meal the one who was to betray Jesus was identified, but the means by which Jesus did it is different between the three synoptics and *According to John*.

Both by the context and by the words of explanation, Paul emphasizes the function of the eating and drinking to be the corporate proclamation of the death of the Lord until he comes. It also cements the believers as members of the body of the crucified, ties the believers to the object of their faith, makes the cross a present event, and connects the Lord's Supper to the baptism of believers. Paul understands baptism as the means by which a human being participates in the death and the resurrection of Christ. His question to the romans is: "Do you not know that all of us who have been baptized into Christ Jesus were baptized into his death?" (Rom. 6:3). Paul does not see baptism as accomplishing the forgiveness of sins, but a death, a burial and a resurrection with Christ. It is the means by which an individual ceases to live in the world of Adam and begins to live in the world of the Spirit that created the Last Adam at the resurrection of Christ. For Paul, Christ did not die in anybody's stead. He died to destroy the power of sin and the law, and to make it possible for the Spirit to bring about a new creation. Christians are those who participate in the death and the resurrection of Christ, thereby living in the new creation. That is what baptism accomplishes for those who exercise faith in what God did in Christ.

Baptism is a personal experience on the part of believers that makes them members of the body of Christ. The Lord's Supper is what makes a body of the members who have been baptized. By celebrating the Lord's Supper often "in remembrance of me" (1 Cor. 11:25), the Christ who is absent becomes present "between the times." Celebrating the Lord's Supper, Christians actualize a death that took place in the past, making it real until the future coming of the Lord. In this first report of the Lord's Supper known to us, the emphasis is not placed in the bread and the wine, or the fact that the Lord will not be able to drink the fruit of the vine until the apocalyptic kingdom is established. It makes the point that the meal is the bond that makes and keeps the community. It exists to proclaim the saving action of God in Christ, making the members an organic functioning body that objectifies Christ in the world between his resurrection and his *Parousia*. It is only at the beginning of the second century that the celebration of the Lord's Supper was given a salvific function and the bread and the wine became the center of attention. Ignatius of Antioch, around 110 C.E., described the bread and the wine as the "medicine of immortality" thus initiating the process that turned the elements of the meal into sacred objects (Ignatius, *To the Ephesians*, 20).

Paul next discusses the need for the members of the body of Christ to celebrate the Lord's Supper in a way fitting the reality being represented by the meal. He thinks that the way in which the Corinthians are celebrating the meal is establishing the differences between the rich and the poor instead of fostering the unity of the members of the body. Describing their meal, he writes, "in eating, each one goes ahead with his own meal, and one is hungry and another is drunk" (1 Cor. 11:19 – 20). His advice to them is quite revealing. "Anyone who unworthily eats the bread or drinks the cup of the Lord becomes guilty of the body and the blood of the Lord" (1 Cor. 11:27, my translation). To participate of the Lord's Supper unworthily is to do so when one is not a member of the body which the Supper energizes. Paul has just told the Corinthians: "As often as you eat this bread and drink the cup, you proclaim the Lord's death until he comes" (1Cor. 11:26). Rather than to proclaim that the crucifixion is the gateway to salvation, those who partake of it without being members of the body, proclaim themselves guilty of the crucifixion, something which Paul declares "the rulers of this world," that is, the principalities and powers of the air, are guilty of (1 Cor. 2:8). In this way, Paul identifies those who partake of the Supper unworthily, on account of their failure to take seriously the body which the Supper energizes, as servants of demons.

The meal establishes that those participating are living within a continuum in time which defines their existence between the death of the Lord and his *Parousia*. In other words, the meal places them in the course of salvation history and defines them as members of the body of Christ. In view of the significance of the meal, Paul then declares, "any one who eats and drinks without discerning the body eats and drinks judgment upon himself" (1 Cor. 11:29). To think that one is a member of the body of Christ while not "discerning the body" to which one claims to belong is to be, at best, naive, and at worst a hypocrite. These words do not make reference to the nature of the bread being eaten, but to the nature of the Christian community. To be a member of the body of Christ requires conscious discernment of one's own purpose for living in the world. The church is a community in which God appoints apostles, prophets, teachers, workers of miracles, healers, helpers, administrators and speakers in various tongues (1 Cor. 12:28) in order to make effective Christ's presence in the world. Paul introduces this fact by telling the Corinthians, "Now you are the body of Christ and individually members of it" (1 Cor. 12:27). The function of the body of Christ is to make him present in society, and the only reason for celebrating the Lord's Supper is to consolidate that body. Thus, those not conscious of the body which the Supper sustains are not members of it. By eating and drinking at the Lord's Supper, they do not bring Christ to the world but judgment upon themselves.

To all appearances, in the interval between the crucifixion and the *Parousia* Christ is not present in the world. But that is not quite true. The Risen Christ is very much present in as much as the sum of the members in the Christian community are his body. Paul conceives the body of Christ in a very concrete and compelling way. Since the body is what gives a living being objective reality and the ability to relate to other human beings, the community of those who live in Christ makes possible the participation of the Risen Christ in the lives of men and women. This is quite different from the way in which the body of the Risen Christ is understood in *To the Colossians*. There the whole of the universe, the totality of all that exists, the *Pleroma*, is the body of the Risen Christ (Col. 1:19; 2:9). Whereas in *To the Colossians* the Risen Christ's body is a cosmic reality, in the letters of Paul it is a social reality that demonstrates the love of God to the world.

As members of the body of Christ, who seat together at the table of the Lord and eat his body and drink his blood, Christians must consider whether their lives actually make the Lord present in the world. They must constantly be aware of whose life they are objectifying in the world. What Paul says about Christians who feel able to eat two breads and thereby become "partners with demons" (1 Cor. 10:20), he also says about the Christian who joins his body to that of a prostitute and becomes one body with her (1 Cor. 6:16). Considering this situation, Paul asks the Corinthians who say "all things are lawful for me," "Do you not know that your bodies are members of Christ?" (1 Cor. 6:15). According to him, "the body is not meant for immorality, but for the Lord, and the Lord for the body" (1 Cor. 6:13). This is a perplexing statement unless one realizes that the body is the way in which a life is objectified in the world. As the body of Christ, Christians live in order to objectify the Risen Lord in the world, and the Lord wishes to be present in the world through the bodies of those who have been created as new persons by the same Spirit that raised Christ from the dead.

Those who live as manifestations of the power that raised the Living Christ from the dead are described by Paul as members of the body that is the temple of the Holy Spirit that dwells in them. By means of this image Paul ties each Christian to the Risen Christ. In antiquity temples were miniatures of the cosmic structure of a given culture. They could not be located arbitrarily. They were built in places that were conceived as central to the cosmic structure. They were manageable representations of the universe that made communication between the gods and their human servants possible. The energy of the universe flowed through the temple. The shedding of the blood of sacrificial offerings energized the divine world above and placated the anger of the gods of the underworld.

The Priestly account of creation (Gen. 1:1 – 2:4) already dislocated the temple from a geographic location considered to be of axial significance by establishing the Sabbath day as the temple through which God and the created human world keep in touch. The Sabbath transfers the umbilical cord that connects and transmits energy between the divine and the human spheres from geographical space to a marker in time. By resting on the Sabbath humans repeat what God did at the beginning. As a temple in time, the Sabbath was a theological breakthrough for a people who were destined to live dispersed throughout the world. Paul and the gospel *According to John* dislocate the temple from geographical bonds even further. The gospel takes worship away from both Mt. Gerizim and Mt. Zion and proclaims, "God is spirit, and those who worship him must worship in spirit and in truth" (Jn. 4:24). Paul proclaims the body of Christian believers a temple of the Holy Spirit. The spirit that created the Risen Christ dwells in this temple. Because of this, each Christian must be careful to "discern the body" and glorify God in the body. They are members of the body that is the miniature representation of the new creation and makes communication with the divine possible; they are the umbilical cord through which communication with God is channeled. By describing the community of Christians as a temple, Paul demonstrates that at the center of his theological horizon is the new creation of the Risen Christ. As the miniature representing the schema of the new creation, the body of Christian believers prefigures the reality of the final triumph of God when all those who are in Christ will receive their spirit bodies. For now, they are the temple of the Holy Spirit (1 Cor. 6:19). Only those who "discern the body" are members of the body of Christ, building blocks of the temple that facilitates the presence of Christ in the world and the glorification of God in the present evil age.

XIII. I Have Made Myself a Slave to All

Slaves of divinities were quite common in the Hellenistic world. The slave girl at Philippi who followed Paul and Barnabas for several days shouting "These men are servants [slaves] of the Most High God" was not dismissed as a charlatan by her audience. Her story reveals to us that what she said was accepted as normal (Acts 16:17). The *Satyricon* of Petronius, a contemporary of Paul, tells the adventures of Encolpius, a slave of Priapus, the god of male sexual prowess. Some consider this tale the forerunner of the novel as a literary form. In his letters, Paul insists that he is an apostle of Jesus Christ, but he defines his apostleship as a form of slavery. This is remarkable because Paul lived in a society where slavery was institutionalized, and most likely he came from a family that owned slaves. As a child of a Jewish upper middle-class family of the Diaspora, Paul must have come into close contact with family slaves. Depending on how old he was when he left home to study at Jerusalem, most likely after having reached a certain age he exercised the master's authority over slaves. Since childhood he must have enjoyed the benefits of having household slaves performing the tasks that allowed the family members to live more comfortably. Paul's reference to the differences in status between minors, adults and household slaves may reflect personal recollections (Gal. 3:25; 4:2). If his life had followed the course to which he seemed destined by birth and upbringing, he would have been among the master class in Hellenistic society. His social prejudices, in spite of his Christian conversion, show him a man of the upper class, well educated, literate, with certain condescending attitudes toward manual labor, and not particularly concerned with slavery as a social evil or a human injustice.

A very large proportion of the population of the Roman Empire consisted of slaves who served earthly masters in all kinds of work, from dirty miners working underground to philosophers who were tutors of the young in wealthy homes. Paul does not condemn the institution that places them in that status within society. He declares that any one of them who is called by Christ is a "freedman of the Lord" (1 Cor. 7:20). "In the flesh," however, they may remain slaves to their earthly masters.

It happened that Paul was not to be a master of slaves. His encounter with the Risen Christ did not bring about a change of the God to be worshiped but a change of vocation. Once he realized that God had raised the crucified from the dead (1 Cor. 6:14; 2 Cor. 4:14), and that the Risen Christ is now in the process of bringing all things in the universe into subjection to himself (Phil. 3:21) in order to be able to deliver all things to the overall dominion of God (1 Cor. 15:28), Paul immediately placed himself under God and Christ's dominion as a faithful slave (2 Cor. 10:5; Gal. 1:10). Having received the call to be an apostle for Christ, he found his Master and became a slave not only of God but of all women and men as well. Thus, for him, Christ became "My Lord" (Phil. 3:8).

In Aramaic "Adonai" means "My Lord." Wherever the Hebrew Scriptures has Yahve, Jews eager not to transgress the second commandment, forbidding the use of the name of God in vain, read "Adonai." The Greek translation of the Scriptures used in the Hellenistic synagogues, the Septuagint, had translated Yahve as *Kyrios*, Lord. When Paul refers to passages of Scripture, either quoting or paraphrasing, he consistently designates Yahve as *Kyrios*. When he is writing on his own, not referring to a Scriptural passage, Paul also designates God as *Kyrios* (1 Cor. 10:9, 22; 1 Th. 4:6). Usually, however, *Kyrios* designates Jesus Christ, but in a few instances it is difficult to determine whether the term designates God or Christ (i.e., 2 Cor. 3:16; 5:11).

Meditations on the Letters of Paul 143

The confession "Jesus Christ is Lord" was already well established among Christians before Paul's conversion. It is the culmination of the hymn to Christ quoted by Paul in *To the Philippians* (2:5 – 11). Throughout his letters, Paul makes clear that Christians live attached to their Lord. It is essential to have a Lord, and for Christians it can only be Jesus Christ. To believe in heart and mind that Christ is Lord and to confess him such with the lips is the clear sign that the Gospel has effectively exercised its power to save (Rom. 10:9).

The pagans who became Christians surely found the designation of Christ as Lord quite appropriate. In their religious world the pagan gods were known as Lord Serapis, Lord Osiris, Lord Dionysius, etc. The notion that they were to submit to the Lord Jesus Christ was not at all a strange idea. For Paul to understand Jesus Christ as Lord was quite congenial to his vision of the world as existing under the power of cosmic forces that are struggling for control over the affairs of the world. For him the decisive battle in the struggle had already been fought. The victor was the Risen Christ who, therefore, could truthfully be acclaimed as Lord. The god of this world (2 Cor. 4:4), Satan (2 Cor. 2:11; 11:14), had been defeated. The love (Rom 5:8) and the power (1 Cor. 6:4) of God have brought about a new creation in which "Jesus Christ is our Lord" (1 Cor. 1:8; 5:5; 2 Cor. 8:9; 1 Th. 2:19; Phil. 3:20). Christians no longer live in the creation where Satan, the god of this world, reigns by the power of sin and death.

As creatures in the world humans have only two options. Jesus Christ is the Lord of those who belong to the Christian community, whereas, unbelievers live under the power of other lords (1 Cor. 8:5) and demons (1 Cor. 10:25). Human beings are either slaves of sin or slaves of righteousness (Rom. 6:16 – 17). It may be possible for some to hide the identity of the lord they serve. Slaves of Satan may succeed in disguising themselves as slaves of righteousness (2 Cor. 11:15). In this they are just following the example of their lord, who is guile personified. He pretends to be an angel of light, but the disguise of the master deceiver and his slaves will be exposed when at the end they will be judged according to their deeds.

The slaves of the Lord Jesus Christ follow the example of their Lord. Their Lord, even though he was in the form of God, took the form of a slave and was obedient unto death (Phil. 2:6 – 7). For Paul, this is the example to be followed. The Lord is the one who destroyed the power of sin and death. As his apostle, Paul is not a junior lord, but a slave. Christ's lordship by the power of Him who raised him from the dead was predicated on his having been obedient unto death on a cross. Paul chose to become a slave and live crucified with Christ (Gal. 2:20), dying daily for the sake of others (1 Cor. 15:31), so as to live with Christ as a slave at the service of all women and men (2 Cor. 4:5).

Only those who join Christ in his death and resurrection can, as participants in the new creation, live as slaves of righteousness. They are enslaved to the authority and the power that creates and gives life. That is the task of the slaves of the God who saves. Paul had experienced the power that saves and understood that the experience had given him a new vocation: to extend to others the power of the Gospel that saves. That could not be done by competing lords. It could be done only by obedient slaves.

Good slaves are at all times conscious of their Lord. Paul insists that whatever Christians are and everything Christians do they ought to be and do "in the Lord Jesus Christ." Paul's apostleship is "in the Lord" (1 Cor. 9:2). Those who are in charge of the churches are leaders "in the Lord" (1 Th. 5:12; 2 Cor. 10:8; 13:10). Tryphaena and Tryphosa are "workers in the Lord" and the beloved Persis has "worked hard in the Lord," while Rufus is "eminent in the Lord" (Rom. 16:12, 13). In the family of Narcissus, apparently, some are "in the Lord" while others are not (Rom. 16:11).

Paul's authority is "in the Lord" (2 Cor. 10:8; 13:10). His comings and goings are "in the Lord" (2 Cor. 2:12). Whatever confidence he has in the members of his congregations is "in the Lord" (Gal. 5:10). What he is sure of, "he knows and is persuaded in the Lord" (Rom. 14:14). It is "in the Lord" that he instructs, exhorts, or commands his converts (1 Th. 4:1).

The saints ought to do things "in the Lord" (Rom. 16:2). They are "elect in the Lord" (Rom. 16:13). They have been "called in the Lord" (1 Cor. 7:22). Their "faith . . . love . . . and hope is in the Lord" (1 Th. 1:3). They are expected to "stand firm in the Lord" (Phil. 4:1; 1 Th. 3:8). They must have the same mind "in the Lord" (Phil. 4:2). Above all, they must always "rejoice in the Lord" (Phil. 3:1; 4:4). In a word, Christians live "in the Lord" (Rom. 14:4). The Pauline epigram sums it up, "As therefore you received Christ Jesus the Lord, so live in him" (Col. 2:6).

Those who live in the Lord are under his dominion. They have been transferred from the dominion of sin and death and live under the rule of Christ. Moreover, those who live as slaves of sin (Rom. 6:17, 20), captives of the law of sin and death (Rom. 7:6, 23; 8:2; Gal. 3:23), in bondage to "weak and beggarly elemental spirits" (Gal. 4:8), need not live in that servitude. Life in Christ means deliverance from the dominion of death. Christians live serving Christ in the new life of the Spirit (Rom. 7:6).

As already pointed out, creatures are not absolutely free. As creatures, their options are slavery to the power of sin that brings about death or slavery to the power of the Gospel that gives life. Under the Lord Jesus Christ, Christians live the life assigned to them (1 Cor. 7:17), but this does not make them into mindless robots lacking individuality. The power that gives life has one source, the Spirit, but the Spirit does not energize everyone to do the same thing, or to behave in unison. The power of the Spirit that gives life to the slaves of Christ is manifested in the diversity to be found among those who are "in the Lord." Unlike slavery to the law which demands the same from everyone and empowers death over all, service to Christ is characterized by "righteousness and peace and joy in the Holy Spirit. He who thus serves Christ is acceptable to God and approved by men" (Rom. 14:17).

Empowered by the Spirit, those who serve Christ are endowed with a great diversity of gifts in order to function in various capacities for the benefit of their fellows. As a slave to all women and men, Paul is not under the dominion of others. As a slave of the Lord who constrains him to be an agent of the love of God, Paul considers his slavery not bondage but freedom. Being a slave of his Lord is to be free because all slaves of the Lord are empowered by the Spirit, and "where the Spirit of the Lord is, there is freedom" (2 Cor. 3:17). When slaves are empowered by the Spirit of the Risen Christ who brought about a new creation, their slavery is freedom from the power of the "elemental spirits" of the world and the law of sin and death. Free from the bondage of the law that demands the same from everybody, the slaves of the Lord Jesus Christ are free to develop their God-given gifts, the fruit of the Spirit, with imagination and creativity. In Paul's apocalyptic symbolic universe, creatures are not free agents operating in a power vacuum. They are in bondage either to the power of sin and death or to the power of the Spirit of life. It is only when life is powered by the Spirit that freedom from the death demanded by the law, the ultimate enemy, becomes a reality. This gives the slaves of the Lord peace and joy in the life they still live in the flesh.

XIV  THE CREATION ITSELF WILL BE SET FREE

During his ministry, Paul found that often his converts turned to either very conservative or very libertine versions of the Gospel that were preached by other apostles. The Corinthians had been taught that once they were baptized with Christ they had already escaped the world of the flesh and were living in the Spirit. What they did with their bodies was no longer significant. They were free to eat at the table of pagan temples, they could have intercourse with prostitutes, they were free spirits for whom "all things are lawful." Paul found their freedom to be a denial of the lordship of Christ in their lives. To them he wrote, "You were bought with a price, do not become slaves of men" (1 Cor. 7:23). Having accepted what they had been taught by other Christian missionaries, as far as Paul was concerned they had become slaves of men because their 'gospel' was not liberating. What they sold as freedom was a surrender to worldly passions.

In *To the Galatians* Paul is at the end of his wits, exasperated, frustrated with the addressees and angry with those who "trouble" them. Toward the end of the letter he took the papyrus and the pen from his scribe to make sure that they would take him seriously. He ends the letter writing, "Henceforth let no man trouble me" (Gal. 6:17). Most scholars date *To the Galatians* as one of the earliest letters of Paul. I am inclined to think that it was written toward the end of his ministry. Paul is evidently tired of being misrepresented and persecuted. He has reached the limit of his patience with those who make him the constant object of their attacks. He refers to them saying, "there are some who trouble you and want to pervert the gospel of Christ" (Gal. 1:7); later, in the body of the letter he says, "he who is troubling you will bear his judgment, whoever he is" (Gal. 5:10). Earlier he had said, "You were running well," and asked, "Who hindered you from obeying the truth?" (Gal. 5:7). We can sense Paul's heavy heart when in this letter he tells his audience three times that what is at stake is the truth of the Gospel (Gal. 2:14; 4:16; 5:7). Paul's ire is against those who insist that God's covenant with the people of Israel at Sinai is still in effect and, therefore, Christians must live under the law like the Jews have lived since the Exodus from Egypt. Paul had preached the Gospel to them and they had received the Spirit as confirmation that the power of the Gospel was at work in their lives (Gal. 3:2 – 3). On the strength of this evidence Paul says that they had been running well. Now they had been listening to other apostles who told them that they had to "live like Jews" (Gal. 2:14). Paul considered their conduct a return to slavery.

According to Paul the issue is whether life as a Christian is life in slavery or life in freedom. If Christians live under the law or under the desires of the flesh, they have not been liberated by the Gospel. Imposing obedience to the law as the Christian way of life, or denying the Lordship of the Risen Christ, is to affirm that the death and the resurrection of Christ was nothing more than a Roman execution. In such case, in Paul's words, "Christ died to no purpose" (Gal. 2:21). Rehearsing their personal trajectory as Gentiles, Paul tells them, "Formerly, when you did not know God, you were in bondage to beings that by nature are no gods, but now that you have come to know God, or rather to be known by God, how can you turn back again to the weak and beggarly elemental spirits, whose slaves you want to be once more?" (Gal. 4:8 – 9). This is an extraordinary passage; in it Paul equates idolatry, bondage to beings who by nature are no gods, to living under the law, which is bondage to the law of Moses. In his view these are equally counterproductive. He regards the law of Moses as a "weak and beggarly elemental spirit"; moreover, those who think that to be Christians they must be circumcised and become Jews are in a condition like that of pagans who worship idols.

To establish the legitimacy of his understanding of the Gospel, Paul tells of his trip to Jerusalem seventeen years after his encounter with Christ. He had gone with Barnabas and Titus, and the pillars of the Christian movement in Jerusalem agreed that Titus, who was a Gentile, did not need to be circumcised. Other Christians, "false brethren," however, "slipped in to spy our freedom which we have in Christ Jesus, that they might bring us into bondage" (Gal. 2:4). To Paul, these are the alternatives: either freedom in Christ or bondage under the law. With the support of James, Cephas and John, Paul reports that he and Barnabas "did not yield submission to them [those who wished to bring them into bondage] even for a moment, that the truth of the gospel might be preserved" for all Gentiles (Gal. 2:5). Freedom from life under the law is freedom from sin as defined by the law, that is, "our freedom which we have in Christ Jesus." Paul spends all his energies "to preserve the truth of the Gospel," that is, to defend the freedom Christians have in Christ Jesus.

As elaborated in a previous meditation, in *To the Romans* Paul argues to his fellow Jews that while it is true that Abraham is "the father of us all," the sons of Abraham are those who like Abraham have faith in God, not those who are descendants of Abraham according to the flesh. In *To the Galatians,* Paul is writing to Gentiles. To them, he argues first that the law of Moses did not nullify the promise God had given to Abraham 430 years earlier (Gal. 3:17). He points out, moreover, that the promise was made to Abraham and to his seed, and his seed is Christ. Now, God sent Christ "to redeem those who were under the law, so that we might receive adoption as sons" (Gal. 4:5). He continues, "So through God you are no longer a slave but a son" (Gal. 4:7). To further identify the sons of Abraham, Paul then introduces a second argument by allegorizing another aspect of Abraham's life, which is built on the understanding that you are a Jew if your mother is a Jewish woman.

It serves Paul to highlight what for him is essential: a gospel that does not bring about freedom is no Gospel at all.

Paul reminds the Galatians who "desire to be under the law" that "Abraham had two sons, one by a slave and one by a free woman. But the son of the slave was born according to the flesh, the son of the free woman through promise" (Gal. 4:21 – 23). Paul then explains that the story of the two women who gave sons to Abraham does not merely tell about something that happened centuries ago. It is also an allegory that says something about the present situation. Paul points out that while the son of Hagar was born "according to the flesh," that is in the natural course of events, the son of Sarah was born "through promise." Isaac was not the product of marital love, but of a promise of God. As Paul emphasizes elsewhere, when God promised Abraham a son Sarah was barren and Abraham was "as good as dead" sexually (Rom. 4:19). Since Hagar was a slave, Ishmael was born a slave. Since Sarah was a free woman, Isaac, the son "through promise," was born a free man.

Paul is now ready to draw out his allegorical interpretation of the story. He states it bluntly. "These women are two covenants" (Gal. 4:24). One covenant is represented by Hagar who gave birth to a slave child. This is the covenant established on Mt. Sinai in Arabia, and "corresponds to the present Jerusalem, for she is in slavery with her children" (Gal. 4:25). The lining up of Hagar with Sinai is rather surprising because in *To the Romans* Paul says that to the Israelites "belong the sonship, the glory, the covenants, the giving of the law, the worship, and the promises" (Rom. 9:4), leaving no doubt that the possession of these benefits was a great blessing.

This listing speaks of "the covenants" and "the promises" — both in the plural. Paul does not think of Sinai as a re-enactment of the covenant with Abraham, and does not relate the promise of a dynasty to David to the promise of descendants to Abraham. This may seem a bit surprising, even confusing. Even more surprising is that in his heated rebuke to the Galatians, Paul lines up Hagar and Sinai as originators of slavery, saying that those who entered into a covenant with God were enslaved. This is surprising, however, only until one realizes that Paul is saying it to establish a basis for the application of the allegory to the situation with which he is dealing.

The "real" sons of Hagar, who are children "according to the flesh," and are slaves of the Sinai law, it turns out, are the leaders of the Christian movement, the "present Jerusalem, for she is in slavery with her children" (Gal. 4:25). Obviously, Paul is not referring to the Jews who worship at the temple in Jerusalem. He is referring to the Christians in Jerusalem who tried to enslave Titus back then and are trying to enslave the Galatians now by obliging them to be circumcised and become Jews who live under the law, enslaved to the covenant ratified at Sinai.

"But the Jerusalem above is free, and she is our mother. . . . Now we, brethren, like Isaac, are children of promise" (Gal. 4:26, 28). Christians who accept Paul's gospel are children of the free woman. Again we are surprised by Paul. Sarah, who is not mentioned by name, represents the covenant ratified at "the Jerusalem above." The children of promise, who are free women and men, don't live under a covenant ratified on earth, according to the flesh. They are bound by a covenant established by a divine promise that issues from "the Jerusalem above." This is the new covenant that only the Spirit can ratify. It is the covenant that sets its members free from enslavement of the law.

Finally, Paul gives to the allegory a personal application. "As at that time he who was born according to the flesh persecuted him who was born according to the Spirit, so it is now" (Gal. 4:29). Those who persecuted Paul were not zealous Jews who were expelling Christians from their synagogues. They were zealous Christians who disapproved Paul's Gospel of the radical opening of the grace of God toward all humanity and placed Jews and Gentiles on an equal footing before God. Apparently, those who wanted to circumcise the Galatians had told them that Paul actually taught that circumcision and the keeping of the law was still a requirement of all those who wanted to be in a covenant relationship with God (Gal. 5:11). They must have sensed the high esteem in which Paul was held by his converts and for this reason told these converts that Paul agreed with them, or at least suggested that he did.

Paul, obviously, became very upset hearing what had been said about his position on the matter. His animosity toward anyone who would describe his preaching in those terms is shown by the very blunt way in which he encourages them to use the circumcision knife. He starts the attack with one of his well hewn rhetorical questions, "If I, brethren, still preach circumcision, why am I still persecuted? In that case the stumbling block of the cross has been removed." Contemplating this disfiguration of his preaching, Paul explodes, "I wish those who unsettle you would mutilate themselves!" (Gal. 5:11 – 12). Undoubtedly, he is *still* being persecuted after having been preaching his Gospel for over a decade with the approval of the "pillars" in Jerusalem. This is happening because he preaches the freedom from the law enjoyed by those living in the new creation. Those who persecute him have removed the stumbling block of the cross denying its effectiveness as the agent of freedom. They fail to realize its significance as the end of the power of the law as the agent of condemnation.

As pointed out in another meditation, explaining why it is not true that God failed to keep his promise to Israel, Paul quotes the words of Isaiah saying that God is placing a precious cornerstone in Zion that will establish believers (Is. 28:16). Paul explains that this precious stone which was intended as a stepping stone to believers became a stumbling stone to the Jews because they "pursued the righteousness which is based on law" (Rom. 9:31). Trying to establish their righteousness on the basis of works, the Jews stumbled on the cross of Christ, the block placed by God as a stepping stone. This allows Paul to argue that the fault for the Jews having failed to obtain righteousness was not God's but theirs. Writing to the romans, Paul understands that, as Isaiah said, the stone placed by God was to serve a good purpose. Now writing to the Galatians, he still insists that even as a stumbling stone, rather than a stepping stone, the stone placed by God serves a positive role. The cross of Christ is the stumbling stone on which people must exercise faith in God's saving action. As such, it cannot be removed. Those Christians who insist that righteousness is to be based on the law of Moses remove the stumbling stone which God has intended as the test of the righteousness by faith. Not only that, they persecute those who like Paul preach the Gospel of freedom from the law, sin and death.

The freedom that characterizes the new creation was the fulfillment of the promise to Abraham that his descendants were to be as numerous as the stars of the heavens and the sands of the sea. Paul recognized that before the cross and the resurrection of Christ Jews had been the beneficiaries of a special relationship with God, and circumcision was the marker of that relationship. As far as Paul was concerned, to fail to recognize the death and the resurrection of Christ as what established the new creation, and to insist on living under the covenant established at Mt. Sinai with the Israelites, is to "nullify the grace of God" (Gal. 2:21). Paul summarizes his argument to the Galatians, "For neither circumcision counts for anything, nor uncircumcision, but a new creation" (Gal. 6:15).

Paul draws the conclusion of the allegory of the two women who bore children to Abraham with the words, "So, brethren, we are not children of the slave but of the free woman. For freedom Christ has set us free. Stand fast therefore, and do not submit again to a yoke of slavery" (Gal. 4:31 – 5:1). Those who live in Christ have been freed from slavery to the beings who by nature are no gods, that is, idolatry, as well as from the law ratified at Sinai. They are rightful heirs of Abraham on account of their being children of promise who are engendered in freedom by the Spirit. They are bound in a covenant made in the Jerusalem above.

In *To the Corinthians II* Paul also says, "If any one is in Christ, he is a new creation" (2 Cor. 5:17). Earlier in the letter he had described "the dispensation of the Spirit" (2 Cor. 3:8). In this dispensation Christ unveils the minds of people so that they are liberated from the traditional way of reading Moses as a law that is binding on those who live in the dispensation of the Spirit. Then Paul redefines the dispensation of the Spirit saying, "Now the Lord is the Spirit, and where the Spirit of the Lord is, there is freedom" (2 Cor. 3:17). For Paul, the life of the Christian is life in freedom, even while living "in the flesh," because the Christian is no longer under the law and therefore no longer under the power of sin as defined by the law that divides humanity into Jews and Gentiles. Of course, Christians are not at all under the power of the principalities and powers of the air, beings which by nature are no gods. Therefore, Paul is free "to become all things to all men, that I might by all means save some" (1 Cor. 9:22). He sets up this affirmation with a description. "For though I am free from all men, I have made myself a slave to all" (1 Cor. 9:19). Paul believes that freedom is to be used, and he has found ways in which to use the freedom which he has in Christ in the service of others by becoming all things to all men and women.

Christian freedom is not absolute freedom. Contrary to what was claimed by the Corinthians, it does not make "all things lawful." In Paul's apocalyptic symbolic universe only God has pure freedom. He is the one who "names the things that are not as well as the things that are" (Rom. 4:17). He stands in the abyss that separates the created world from the vacuum of non-being. With these words Paul presents a God who controls the uncreated, the realm of pure potentiality, the realm of things not determined. That is the realm where any and every thing is possible. Absolute freedom dwells where actuality is absent. This is the realm of miracles. Christians do not live there; their freedom exists within bounds. In Paul's writings freedom is usually followed by a preposition. Men and women in Christ are free *for*, free *from*, free *to*. They are free *for* righteousness, free *from* the condemnation of the law, free *to* serve God.

Freedom is dependent on power. People are free to the degree of the power that sustains their freedom. Of course, different freedoms require different powers to sustain them. In daily life the powers that sustain freedom are time, health, money, intelligence, natural or disciplined ability, etc. Of course, brute force and military might also are capacitors of freedom both at the personal or the national level. All these powers operate in the world of the flesh, and some may also operate in the world of the Spirit. For Paul, however, humans who live in Christ are endowed with the greatest of freedoms because they are energized by the greatest of powers, the power that raised Christ from the dead and creates new beings out of humans living in the flesh. That is why Paul understands that the Gospel is the power of God at work (Rom. 1:16). The Gospel is not a message, but a power — the power that brings about freedom from death, the last enemy.

Paul warns the Galatians, "You were called to freedom, brethren; only do not use your freedom as an opportunity for the flesh, but through love be servants of one another" (Gal. 5:13). Like Paul's concepts of the body and the flesh, his concept of freedom shares the tensions experienced by those who live in Christ while also living in the flesh. Christians must not use their freedom to satisfy the desires and the passions of the flesh. The needs of others make claims on them, and the love of God constrains them to serve those needs. They are free from sin and death and free to love their fellow humans.

Paul recognizes the contradiction contained in the affirmation that the one who is free in Christ must be a servant of others. He asks the appropriate question when considering the case of a Christian who has accepted an invitation to eat at a friend's house and is informed that the food being served has been offered to an idol. It would seem that something has been lost in the text, because as it reads now it is difficult to follow Paul's reasoning. He says that, out of consideration of the conscience of his friend, the Christian should not eat this food. Had his neighbor not told him that the food had been offered to an idol, having given thanks to God for the food, the Christian would have been free to eat whatever his friend was serving him. In the midst of this illustration Paul asks, "Why should my liberty be determined by another man's scruples?" (1 Cor. 10:29).

The question is most relevant, especially in the way in which it is asked in the original Greek, "Why should my freedom be judged by someone else's conscience?" Paul does say that to defile the weak conscience of a fellow Christian is to sin against Christ (1 Cor. 8:7, 12). On the other hand, Paul also says that the weak in faith who eat only vegetables should not judge those who eat whatever they want to (Rom. 14:2 – 3). It would seem that Paul is making a difference between: a) the conscience of the non-Christian friend (1 Cor. 10:29) or the weak conscience of a fellow Christian (1 Cor. 8:10), and b) the conscience of Christians who are weak in faith but strong in judging others (Rom. 14:1). Paul is aware of the difficulties inherent in this kind of situations, but from what we have from him we cannot quite make out how he recommends dealing with those who wish to stifle the freedom of their fellow Christians. Paul is quite clear on the ability of a Christian empowered by the Spirit to determine the will of God with a clear conscience. In this connection, I find Martin Luther's response to Paul's question quite satisfactory; he found a path in the middle. He says that dealing with weak fellow Christians he would never do anything that offends them. On the other hand, dealing with fellow Christians who condemn his words or his actions when he is quite convinced that he is acting according to the Gospel, he is eager to offend them as openly as he can. Their assumption of power to judge others has not been granted to them by the Gospel (See M. Luther, *The Freedom of the Christian*, lines 938 – 948).

The tensions created within the Christian who is free in Christ and tries to apply the ethic of love when dealing with his fellow human beings are quite real and at times confusing. That is why, as Paul says, "in this hope we were saved" (Rom. 8:24). The salvation of believers has been accomplished by a past event, but ultimately they live it "in hope." This hope, Paul the apocalypticist explains, is for the full "revelation of the sons of God." The tensions of life in the flesh do not affect only human flesh; they affect all flesh, that of animals, of birds and of fish. All "creation waits with eager longing" for the full manifestation of the righteousness of God. At that time "the creation itself will be set free from its bondage to decay and obtain the glorious liberty of the children of God." Those who are in Christ have been saved in the hope of "the redemption of our bodies," when together with all creation they will be set free from the bondage to decay and its ultimate expression in biological death (Rom. 8:19 – 23). Then Christians will experience the freedom for which God created them and will become the full revelation of the God who is absolutely free.

XV. I Press On Toward the Goal

As several of my meditations have shown, Paul understands that living in Christ requires performing a balancing act. Christians live between the times, activating their faith in a past event and their hope in a future one. They live between what God has already done and what God is about to do. They live in Christ, but also in the flesh. They live as slaves of God on account of the freedom for which Christ made them free. They have died with Christ to live in Christ. These figures of speech tell us that Paul understands that Christian living in the present evil age requires the ability to balance multiple tensions. The ultimate tension is that while suffering is unavoidable, Paul commands everyone to "rejoice always" (1 Th. 5:16). He confesses "we rejoice in our sufferings" (Rom. 5:3), "with all our affliction, I am overjoyed" (2 Cor. 7:4). The reason for the joy that characterizes all Christians, it would appear, is that their lives are not a protracted waiting for the release from tensions. They are an exhilarating upward journey that is energized by the Spirit that gives them life. Christian living is a process of maturation that reaches its goal with glorification in a spiritual body. It is not easy living, but purpose full living toward a goal.

The call of God reaches humans by the power of the Gospel. Paul sometimes asks his converts to recall their condition before their call. He tells them, "Formerly, when you did not know God, you were in bondage to beings that by nature are no gods" (Gal. 4:8). They were "slaves of sin" (Rom. 6:20). They were the object of God's wrath. Now, since they have responded to the call of God and have received the Spirit, they have started new lives. As an apostle of the Gospel, Paul sees himself as a woman who gives birth to babies (Gal. 5:19). He also sees himself as a nurse who gives milk to babies (1 Th. 2:7), and as a father who exhorts and encourages his children (1 Th. 2:11). Paul thinks that human beings who become Christians start their new life, no matter what their chronological age, as babies, but he does not expect them to remain babies for long. He expects that they will grow into adulthood, developing into complete persons who are fully capable of handling the vicissitudes that life on earth will surely place before them. For this they have the fellowship of the community and their participation in the Spirit (Phil. 2:1).

In his paean to love as supreme over faith and hope, Paul points out the need to grow in faith to the full measure of adulthood. The poem declares love to be the ultimate goal to be reached because "love never ends" (1 Cor. 13:8). To set forth the supremacy of love, Paul makes some important contrasts. "For our knowledge is imperfect and our prophecy is imperfect, but when the perfect comes the imperfect will pass away" (1 Cor. 13:9 – 10). In the same vein, he writes, "When I was a child, I spoke like a child, I thought like a child, I reasoned like a child; when I became a man, I gave up childish ways" (1 Cor. 13:11). The contrast between the "child" (*nepios*) and the "man" (*aner*) is to underline the need to leave behind attachments characteristic of an earlier stage in life. The entire passage is of a piece: progression from childhood to maturity, from imperfection to perfection, from seeing dimly to seeing clearly, knowing partially to understanding fully. The Christian life is a continuous attempt to reach higher toward adulthood, that is, Christian maturity.

Paul does not refer to the child's dependency, innocence, trustfulness or playfulness as the hallmarks of this stage in life. He refers to the child's talking, thinking and reasoning. As pointed out in another meditation, Paul considers thinking and reasoning determining factors in life. As distinct from the gospels in which childhood is a prized condition, here *nepios* takes a somewhat pejorative meaning. It emphasizes a stage in life when a person is underage, not yet grown up, that is, immature. Paul does not recommend the faith of a child. He values the faith of the adult who does not think or reason like a child. He sets himself up as a "man," an adult, a mature person. The mature adult is referred to by the Greek word *teleios*, perfect, which is derived from the word *telos*, meaning end. The predominant idea is that of development toward an end, toward a goal. Paul's idea of the Christian adulthood is developmental. The idea that life has stages of development was common among the Greek philosophers, particularly the Stoics. This is somewhat in contrast with the way in which the Hebrews understood perfection *(tamim)*, not as a stage in a person's development, but as a state of wholeness, integrity or totality. Working with a Hellenistic view of the matter, Paul envisions the Christian child as striving for maturity, trying to attain to the full measure of faith under the guidance of the Spirit.

Paul perceived that the Corinthians had not made much progress in their new life. He writes to them, "But I, brethren, could not address you as spiritual men but as men of the flesh, as babes in Christ. I fed you milk, not solid food; for you were not ready for it; and even yet you are not ready, for you are still of the flesh. For while there is jealousy and strife among you, are you not of the flesh, and behaving like ordinary men?" (1 Cor. 3:1 – 3). What is he saying here? Is he referring to the content of what he taught them? Is he saying that he could not yet reveal to them the mysteries of the divine activity that are reserved for those with an advance knowledge of their faith? By milk, does he mean the introductory matters needed before the more profound doctrines may be understood? Or, is Paul making a distinction between what is expected of Christians in terms of conduct, of the way in which they live with their fellow human beings?

To answer these questions it is necessary to establish the context of Paul's observation that the Corinthians are still "men of the flesh." Earlier, in 1 Corinthians 1:18 to 2:16, Paul refers to the divisions that have resulted from the formation of groups who follow a preferred preacher. Addressing the Corinthian church as a whole, Paul tells them that ranking the preachers they have heard according to criteria used with teachers of "wisdom" does not work in the body of Christ. Apparently those who had taken favorite preachers as their guides were after wisdom, and were boasting about the wisdom they had already attained (1 Cor. 1:29 ff.; 3:21; 4:7). Paul can only address their attitude with a high degree of sarcasm. "Already you are filled! Already you have become rich! Without us you have become kings!" (1 Cor. 4:8). Their claim to be "spiritual" was denied by their behavior. They were living by the standards of their society, and their conduct was having a most deleterious effect on the congregation.

In this context, Paul feels compelled to expand on the "foolishness" of the preaching of the cross, which he has already declared superior to the wisdom of men (1 Cor. 1:25). This folly is the undoing of all human "wisdom." To be taken into account is that Paul talks about "wisdom" as what makes for living well, just as the Greek philosopher, the lovers of wisdom, were also ultimately concerned with what makes for the good life.

Paul frankly admits that "among the mature (*teleios*) we do impart wisdom, although it is not a wisdom of this age or of the rulers of this age" (1 Cor. 2:6). In other words, the wisdom he imparts is not what passes for wisdom in the fallen creation, or what people who join the mystery cults seek from the elemental spirits who rule the spheres between heaven and earth. It does not consist of cosmological knowledge that insures a safe journey to the higher spheres after death. Neither is it aimed at what makes for a good life in the flesh. What is Paul doing by pointing out that there is wisdom from another source, the wisdom of God? Is he saying that the fundamental teaching of the cross is to be followed by a mystery-like discourse on the structure of the heavens which is reserved for the *teleioi*? Not at all. In fact he had been dropping hints by pointing out that "Christ is the power of God, and the wisdom of God" (1 Cor. 1:24), and by elaborating the idea saying that God made Christ Jesus "our wisdom, our righteousness and sanctification and redemption" (1 Cor. 1:30). The point is that the very preaching of the cross, what is "folly" from the point of view of the flesh, viewed correctly is the divine "wisdom," the sure guide to the mature life.

Essentially, what Paul tells the *teleioi*, the mature, is not different from what he tells everyone: the preaching of the cross is the final demonstration of the righteousness of God that accomplishes the successful advancement of those in Christ through the three stages of the Christian life: 1) righteousness, as the call of God is accepted, 2) sanctification, as the Christian matures in his conduct, and 3) redemption, as the final resurrection to a spirit body. This "secret and hidden wisdom of God" (1 Cor. 2:7) Paul imparts to everyone, not to a select few. It is not esoteric knowledge, but power to live in the new creation.

Paul preaches the word of the cross using "words not taught by human wisdom but taught by the Spirit, interpreting spiritual truths to those who possess the Spirit" (1 Cor. 2:13). By contrast, "The unspiritual man does not receive the gifts of the Spirit of God, for they are folly to him, and he is not able to understand them because they are spiritually discerned" (1 Cor. 2:14). Whether one is a child who can only drink milk or an adult capable of digesting solid food depends on the way in which a person lives in society with others. The Corinthians were not and still are not able to see the wisdom of God in the preaching of the cross because they had not yet transferred their knowledge of the Gospel to a way of being that was worthy of the Gospel; they are still men of the flesh. The *teleioi*, the mature, to whom Paul preaches the divine wisdom are not a select, elite, small group who receives a special revelation.

This was the premise of the mystery religions that offered to their initiates access to esoteric knowledge. In Paul's case the mature are those who are already under the guidance of the Spirit applying their knowledge of the Gospel into a manner of being that reflects the love of God and, therefore, are able to discern spiritual things. The Gospel is proclaimed in its wholeness to all, but it is folly to some and wisdom to others. It is grasped as wisdom only by those who have the Spirit of God in their hearts and enjoy a new source of being for their lives. The problem with the Corinthians is that they claim to be spiritual when in truth they are fleshly; they are living by the standards of the world. As Paul says, their jealousy and strife reveal that the Gospel has not impacted their behavior (1 Cor. 3:3).

All Christians are baptized into Christ and start a new life by the power of the Spirit; therefore, all are pneumatics, and yet some are not. They all can and should recognize God's wisdom and live accordingly, and yet some do not. The Corinthians did not because they fancied themselves to have gained esoteric knowledge available to the few elect, and they boasted of their "wisdom." They proclaimed themselves *teleios*, perfect on account of their acquisition of knowledge, but their claim created strife and jealousy, demonstrating thereby to be *nepios*, immature, or underage. They were not living according to love.

Paul returns to the contrast between the child and the adult in his instructions to the Corinthians who place too much emphasis on the gift of tongues. His advice is: "since you are eager for manifestations of the Spirit, strive to excel in building up the church" (1 Cor. 14:12). Then he tells them, "Brethren, do not be children in your thinking, be babes [*nepios*] in evil, but in thinking be mature [*teleioi*]" (1 Cor. 14:20). Given their interest in spiritual things, particularly the gift of tongues, Paul encourages them to use their mind in order to get a clear sense of the variety of the gifts of the Spirit. This means that they should not think like children when they reflect on the gifts. They must become mature, but remain underage in respect to evil, not by being naïve about it, but by not practicing it. In matters of the Spirit they must outgrow the childhood stage and behave compelled by God's love. If their thinking is mature they will realize that speaking in tongues is not an effective way to build up the church which values the mind of Christ.

To the Corinthians who think that Christianity, like the mystery cults that provide worldly wisdom, has to do with esoteric knowledge, Paul makes clear that Christianity is not a matter of knowledge. Christian maturity is a matter of speaking, thinking and reasoning (1 Cor. 13:11) which is activated into patterns of behavior. Paul usually refers to living using the Greek word *peripateo*, "walking around" (Rom. 6:4; 13:13; 2 Cor. 5:7; 10:3). To the Philippians he says, "Only let your manner of life be worthy of the gospel of Christ" (Phil. 1:27). The Greek word translated "manner of life" is *politeuo*. It refers to the life of freedom enjoyed by citizens who participate in the conversations of the urban assemblies with the right to vote. What differentiates the "babes" from the "adults" is not how much they know about the mysteries of God. It is how much, by thinking and reasoning guided by the Spirit, they have been able to process what they know into a manner of life in society as responsible citizens. As such they must live in a manner worthy of the Gospel that reveals the righteousness of God in the cross of Christ. Thinking the cross of Christ is folly aborts the process that makes it the power for living the mature life.

Paul's appeal to the Corinthians to become mature spiritual adults serves as a refrain for his dealing with the various problems affecting the congregation. The existence of cliques, strife, and jealousy are transforming common meals into anything but celebrations of the Lord's Supper. Besides, there are other issues that prove their being babes: a man is living with his father's wife, some members have taken their fellow members to civil courts to resolve disputes, men are visiting prostitutes, and some are eating at pagan temples. None of these are on the surface matters of doctrine. They are what prove that the Corinthians are not "spiritual." Those who are involved in these activities think like children.

Unlike other Christians who require perfection in the obedience to the commandments and conceive of obedience as a state of wholeness, Paul understands that Christians still live in the flesh. However, they must not remain babies; they must strive toward maturity. To the Romans he says, "But thanks be to God, that you who were once slaves of sin have become obedient from the heart to the standards of teaching to which you were committed, and, having been set free from sin, have become slaves of righteousness" (Rom. 6:17 – 18). This transferal of slaveries was achieved when "we were buried with him by baptism . . . into death, so that as Christ was raised from the dead by the glory of the Father, we too might walk in newness of life" (Rom 6:4). "Walking around" in newness of life is the proof that a person is a Christian. As Paul considers the struggles of his ministry, he writes, "Though our outer nature is wasting away, our inner nature is being renewed every day" (2 Cor. 4:16). The word "nature," which brings with it heavy connotations from the history of theology and philosophy, is not from Paul. Here he speaks of the inner and the outer "man" (*anthropos*). The outer person is to be spent at the service of one's neighbors. The inner person is in a daily process of renewal by the power of the Spirit that guides the person to determine what is the good, acceptable and perfect will of God (Rom. 12:2 – 3). That will must then be made effective by the way one "walks around."

Pointing out that "the appointed time has grown very short," Paul tells the Corinthians to live following the "as though" rule. "Let those who have wives live as though they had none, and those who mourn as though they were not mourning, and those who rejoice as though they were not rejoicing, and those who buy as though they had no goods, and those who deal with the world as though they had no dealings with it" (1 Cor. 7:29 – 31). Certainly what Paul is saying is not that Christians should be unfaithful to their wives, hypocritical as to their feelings, liars about their business affairs and devious about their conduct in society. This is, rather, his way of presenting the mature way of living in the world. It recognizes that the one attached to spiritual things is in tension with life in the flesh. Living in the world of the flesh Christians must be conscious that they do not live according to fleshly standards. They cannot give ultimacy to life in this age. Still, they must identify with those living in the flesh "as though" they also lived just in the flesh, in the same way in which, according to Paul, God's son came "in the likeness of" sinful flesh. To be "as though" something is not to be that something. To be "as though" requires mental agility and imagination to identify with others.

Paul's view on the matter becomes clearer in a later passage: "For though I am free from all men, I have made myself a slave to all, that I might win the more. To the Jew I became as a Jew, in order to win Jews; to those under the law I became as one under the law . . . that I might win those under the law. To those outside the law I became as one outside the law . . . that I might win those outside the law. To the weak I became weak, that I might win the weak. I have become all things to all men, that I might by all means save some. I do it all for the sake of the gospel, that I may share in its blessings" (1 Cor. 9:19 – 23). In contrast to the "as though" of Chapter 7, we find here the shorter "as." Of course, to be "as" someone is not to be what that someone is. By the grace of God, Paul was who he was. But for the sake of the righteousness of God revealed at the cross of Christ he became *as* whatever others were in order to win them to the Gospel. This is the conduct of the mature who give ultimate value to spiritual things.

To become as though weeping or as though having a wife, one must know the difference between living in the flesh and living in the Spirit. Only those living in the Spirit know the difference, and they use this knowledge to identify with those who are different from themselves, rather than to consider themselves superior to others. To become *as* a Jew, or *as* one outside the law, is to identify with another on the basis of the power of the love of God demonstrated by Christ at the cross, the love that controls all those who are mature.

There has been no lack of those who see in these words of Paul the evidence for charging him with inconsistency in his conduct, at best, or with outright hypocrisy and spiritual pride, at worst. To do this is to fail to realize the apocalyptic framework of Paul's universe and the way it places Christians who still live in the flesh in tension with the call of Christ to live according to the Spirit as a mature adult in Christ. When the word of the cross has been understood as the wisdom of God, Christians live according to a different source of power. As Paul confesses, "the love of Christ controls us" (2 Cor. 5:14). It is not the case that the "as though," or the "as," rule demands hypocrisy or double talk on the part of Christians. Rather, when Christians experience the renewal of the inner person by the Spirit, they have agile minds that are open to ways of being that give ultimacy to the wisdom of the cross.

The righteousness of God that was effective at the cross and the resurrection, Paul says, "is at work in you, both to will and to work for his good pleasure." In this context, Paul tells the Philippians, "work out your own salvation with fear and trembling" (Phil. 2:12 – 13). The life of Christians "in the midst of a crooked and perverse generation" is one that requires effort, even while God provides both the will and the work necessary to become "lights holding fast the word of life." The word of life, however, is not an intellectual possession. It is what makes Christians "lights" at the service of their fellows. As such, however, they should not think of themselves as models that call attention to themselves. The "blameless and innocent" manner of life (Phil. 2:15) is one that calls attention to the cross of Christ.

The ultimate achievement of the Christian is to "attain the resurrection from the dead" (Phil. 3:11), but only those who have been crucified with Christ will attain it. Probably recalling the claim of the Corinthians to have already achieved it, Paul confesses: "Not that I have already obtained this or am already perfect (*teleios*); but I press on to make it my own, because Christ Jesus has made me his own. Brethren, I do not consider that I have made it my own" (Phil. 3:12 – 13). Paul denies twice that he thinks to have achieved the perfection to be received at the resurrection from the dead. He exerts himself to make the resurrection his own because Christ has made him his own. That is the only legitimate motivation for working out one's own salvation as God provides the will and the work. Only those who know themselves to be owned by Christ Jesus can be obedient from the heart. It is impossible for them to "consider" that they have achieved all that God has to offer. It is because the Corinthians consider that they "possessed all things" and bragged about it that Paul considers them "men of the flesh, babes in Christ."

Meditations on the Letters of Paul

Ancient philosophers disagreed as to whether it was possible for human beings to attain to wisdom. Unlike Plato, who apparently thought that it was possible for true philosophers to attain to wisdom, Socrates considered himself wise precisely because he knew wisdom was unattainable by humans. Only the gods had wisdom. Humans can only be engaged in the pursuit of wisdom. Like Socrates, Paul also understood that it was impossible for humans in this life to attain to full maturity and live the perfect life. The human task is to be engaged in the pursuit of love, however (1 Cor. 14:1). For Socrates wisdom was to be in pursuit of the truth in order to then act accordingly. The task is difficult because truth is hidden under material phenomena. For Paul the wisdom of God, which is folly to the world, is not hidden; it has been revealed in the love of God manifested in the cross and the resurrection that makes possible true life in the Spirit that raised Christ from the dead. The mature Christian who aims to attain to the resurrection of the dead does so by pursuing the love exemplified at the cross, not some hidden truth.

Even as Paul admits not to have arrived he says, "one thing I do, forgetting what lies behind and straining forward to what lies ahead, I press on toward the goal for the prize of the upward call of God in Christ Jesus. Let those of us who are mature (*teleioi*) be thus minded, and if in anything you are otherwise minded, God will reveal that also to you. Only let us hold to what we have attained" (Phil. 3:13 – 16). This is a most revealing confession and admonition. Christians live "straining forward to what lies ahead," the resurrection from the dead. If some Christians do not think so, Paul is confident that God, who is at work in all of them for his own good pleasure, will reveal to them that such is what a Christian life is all about. All Christians are engaged in this effort "toward the goal for the prize of the upward call of God." Again the upward pressing on is in answer to the call of God in Christ who loved all even while they were sinners (Rom. 5:8). It is because God is calling, because Christ has made them his own that Christians find themselves at different stages in their development toward maturity. As Paul concludes his consideration of the matter, he points out the importance of not slipping backwards to an earlier stage. Everyone must "hold to what we have attained." As he tells the Thessalonians, God is eager to have them continually grow in love, not only among the members of the congregation but toward all men (1 Th. 3:12). Growth toward the maturity that expresses itself by loving all men is what must characterize all Christians. If one finds it impossible to advance further, having advanced toward the goal is a victory.

Writing to the Philippians, Paul contrasts the "enemies of the cross of Christ" with the group of apostles to which he belongs. He reminds them that he had warned them about these people before but he has to do it again, even with tears (Phil. 3:17 – 18). He describes the "many" who are enemies of the cross saying that "their end is destruction, their god is their belly, and they glory in their shame, with minds set on earthly things" (Phil. 3:19). These enemies of the cross are not Jews; they are not pagans; they are Christians who insist on a kosher diet (their belly is their god) and glory in their self-righteousness (their shame). In contrast to these Christians, Paul wishes the Philippians to imitate the conduct of his missionary band. The enemies of the cross walk about (*peripateo*) with their minds set on diets and laws (earthly things). Paul makes the contrast saying, "but our civil conversation (*politeuma*) is in heaven" (Phil. 3:20, my translation). The contrast is between having the mind set on earthly things and having in mind set in heaven as one lives responsibly as a citizen in society (*politeia*). The significance of the cross makes real the hope that the Lord Jesus Christ "will change our lowly body to be like his glorious body." Christians live "waiting for" their Savior (Phil. 3:21). The ultimate contrast between the enemies of the cross and those whose civic conversation is in heaven is that while the former will end up destroyed the latter will receive spirit bodies. Paul's words, "but our *politeuma* is in heaven" is usually translated "but our commonwealth is in heaven." These words then become used as evidence for an "other-worldly" Paul. The context, as I have just said, uses them to make a contrast between two ways of being a Christian. As such, they are another way of saying "we live in Christ" or "we live in the Spirit." Paul understands that Christians who live in Christ while living on this earth still live in the flesh and that, therefore, they must carry on a civil conversation in society in a manner worthy of the gospel of Christ. The standard by which they live on earth is in heaven. They live "pressing on" quite aware of the consequences of their conduct. Theirs is not an "other-worldly" existence.

The goal of the Christian, according to Paul, is to receive a body like the glorious body of the Risen Christ at the resurrection of the dead. In the meantime, Christians develop a mind that is not set on earthly things and, therefore, can produce a "walk" that is in accordance with the will of God. God, for his own good pleasure, works in Christians both their will and their work, and guides them by the power of the Spirit so that they progress from glory to glory in an upward development that is led by the call of God. The culmination of their civil conversation will be the reception of a body like the glorious body of the Risen Christ.

XVI. The Day of Christ

One of Paul's most dramatic statements is, "in this hope we were saved" (Rom. 8:24). For him the future is firmly anchored in the past. Were it not so, the future in this present evil age offers no hope. Hope can only be sustained by the power of God demonstrated at the New Creation, the creation of the Son of God at Easter. As we have already noticed several times, faith in the New Creation is the basis of Christian living. The eschatological Son of God, however, has not yet fully accomplished his task. This present Age has given way to the Age of Messiah. But the apocalyptic scenario includes the establishment of the Age to Come. According to Paul, the New Creation has been established, but the fallen creation has not yet been destroyed; therefore, Christians are not quite enjoying full maturity. Their hope is for the soon establishment of the Age to Come at the appearance of the Son of Man in glory.

When Paul gives his "as though" rule, he frames it by saying, "I mean, brethren, the appointed time has grown very short . . . The form of this world is passing away" (1 Cor. 7:29, 31). In his description of the *Parousia* to the Thessalonians he makes it clear that he expects to be alive when the Lord descends from heaven (1 Th. 4:17). Relying on the basic apocalyptic scenario, Paul envisions the Age of Messiah to be a short period of transition between the end of This Age and the coming of the Age to Come. His preaching of the word of the cross aimed to advance the arrival of the Age to Come and the establishment of the kingdom of God. He was "an ambassador for Christ, God making his appeal through us" (2 Cor. 5:20).

Even though God has taken away the kingdom from the powers of evil, these powers still are free in the heavenly spheres and exercise their power over human beings. The purpose of the Age of Messiah is to give Christ time to submit all these powers under his control. Until that is accomplished, God has not taken full dominion over "all things." As soon as Christ completes the subjection of the powers of the air he will deliver "the kingdom to God the Father after destroying every rule and every authority and power. For he must reign until he has put all his enemies under his feet. The last enemy to be destroyed is death . . . When all things are subjected to him [Christ], then the Son himself will also be subjected to him who put all things under him, that God may be everything to every one" (1 Cor. 15:24 – 28). These words show that even though the cross made it possible for Christ to make an inroad into the world of the powers of the spheres that had kept humankind enslaved in sin, it had not brought about their complete demise. Therefore, they continue to exert their power over all those living in the flesh. The resurrection was God's way of exalting Christ above all these powers, without necessarily meaning that Christ had attained effective control over them. The Age of Messiah is the time given to Messiah (Christ) to accomplish the subjugation of the lords of the cosmic spheres; only then "comes the end" (1 Cor. 15:24). Paul's letters fully express his expectations for "that day" (Rom. 13:11 – 14; 1 Cor. 1:7; 7:29, 31; 10:11; Phil. 3:20 f.; 4:5; 1 Th. 4:15), the day of Christ (Phil. 1:10).

On that day those who are dead in Christ and those who are living in Christ, who are being transformed from one degree of glory to another as they advance toward Christian adulthood, will receive ultimate glorification and live in spirit bodies. This means that the resurrection is an essential part of the Day of Christ. Paul argues this fact against the Corinthians who apparently thought that they were raised with Christ at baptism. Their view was based on a docetic understanding of the cross and the resurrection. According to this way of seeing the cross of Christ, Jesus was really a divine being who had taken a human body in the same way in which anyone can put on an overcoat. In other words, the incarnation only made it appear (*dokeo*) that Jesus was a human being. As an immortal divine being it was impossible for him to die. At the crucifixion the divine being left his body for the roman soldiers to carry on their nasty work while he went back to the heavens from where he had come. The mission of this divine being while on earth was to transmit divine knowledge, wisdom, to his audiences. Having accomplished his mission he disposed of his human appearance and later revealed himself to the disciples, without actually having died. That is, he had not actually been raised from death. In order to put things in perspective, Paul begins his discussion of the resurrection by quoting the earliest Christian confession's affirmation of Christ's death. The point is that real resurrection can be only from the dead. To deny the death of Christ is to deny his resurrection, and this is contrary to faith in Christ.

The first step of the argument establishes that there is such a thing as a resurrection from the dead. The argument presupposes that the Corinthians have faith in God as the One who raised Christ. Paul's preaching is nothing other than about God's raising of Christ from the dead. If God did not raise Christ from the dead, Paul has been misrepresenting God and the Corinthians' faith is in vain. If there is no such thing as resurrection from the dead, and Christian hope in Christ is only for life in This Age, Paul concludes, "we are of all men most to be pitied" (1 Cor. 15:12 – 19). The point is that resurrection is not for the continuation of life in the flesh.

The second step in the argument points out that in fact there are two resurrections. The first one establishes the certainty of the second. The resurrection of Christ, established by the first part of the argument, was "the first fruits of those who have fallen asleep" (1 Cor. 15:20). Paul then draws a parallel to argue from the one to the many. "For as in Adam all die, so also in Christ shall all be made alive." In both cases what happened to one happens to many. However, between the resurrection of Christ and that of those who are "in Christ" there is an interval. "Christ, the first fruits, then at his coming those who belong to Christ" (1 Cor. 15:23). Paul reiterates that the resurrection of those in Christ does not happen at their baptism, a past event in the life of the Corinthian Christians, but at the future *coming* of Christ.

To hammer the point in, Paul asks two rhetorical questions: "What do people mean by being baptized on behalf of the dead?" "What do I gain if, humanly speaking, I fought with beasts at Ephesus?" The only reason making sense of someone's baptism on behalf of someone else who has already died, or of Paul's risking his safety facing fierce opponents at Ephesus, is for those being baptized and for Paul, to believe in the future resurrection of those who have died in Christ (1 Cor. 15:29 – 34). Both questions are difficult to interpret. This is the only reference to baptism on behalf of someone already dead; therefore, there is no knowledge of how it was done or of its discrete meaning. The reference to his fighting with beasts at Ephesus is capable of being interpreted literally or metaphorically. It is made in the context of his being "in peril every hour," and is characterized by the phrase "humanly speaking" (*kata anthropon*= according to man). Paul felt that at Ephesus, where he was when he wrote *To the Corinthians I*, he was at risk of dying at the hands of his opponents. He makes a reference to it in 2 Cor. 1:8 – 10. These questions, no doubt, aim to point out not just the fact of a resurrection but the reality of a *future* resurrection.

The final step in the argument addresses the way in which the Corinthians have been ridiculing the notion of the resurrection. It presupposes that all human life is to be lived in a body. Everyone knows that after burial the human body decomposes and, under normal conditions, eventually disappears. Those who deny a future resurrection ask sarcastically, "With what kind of body do they come?" That, says Paul, is a foolish question. Paul affirms the resurrection by making it even more dramatic. The resurrection is not the return to life under the same conditions in which human beings now live. Bodies are the facilitators of life in community, and life in community can take different forms. The resurrection is not a return to earthly existence. It is the portal to existence in a totally different environment. Therefore those who are raised have a "spirit body" rather than a "soul body." The reality of the disintegration of the material body is no argument against the resurrection of the dead. Paul closes the argument declaring, "I tell you this, brethren, flesh and blood cannot inherit the kingdom of God, nor does the perishable inherit the imperishable" (1 Cor. 15:35 – 50). Life after the resurrection is not a return to perishable flesh life.

Paul follows his argument about the future resurrection with the revelation of a "mystery." In antiquity, a mystery was not something that is incapable of rational understanding, but a piece of information that is known by only a few. "Lo! I tell you a mystery. We shall not all sleep, but we shall all be changed, in a moment, in the twinkling of an eye, at the last trumpet. For the trumpet shall sound, and the dead will be raised imperishable, and we shall be changed. For this perishable nature must put on the imperishable, and this mortal nature must put on immortality. When the perishable puts on the imperishable, and the mortal puts on immortality, then shall come to pass the saying that is written: 'Death is swallowed up in victory.' 'O death, where is thy victory? O death, where is thy sting?'" (1 Cor. 15:51 – 55). The ultimate enemy has been vanquished.

No doubt Paul was concerned about death. In his time everyone seems to have known the Stoic maxim "Practice dying." Life is in a constant dance with death. It is notable that Paul considers himself fully alive when he is crucified with Christ. He proclaims, "I die every day" (1 Cor. 15:31). He travels over the Mediterranean world "always carrying in the body the death of Jesus," as he explains, "for while we live we are always being given up to death for Jesus' sake" (2 Cor. 4:10 – 11). Paul's concentration on the death of Christ must be understood in context. Death is the end of the road that begins in sin and is ruled by the law. The alternate road that leads to life begins with the resurrection of Christ from the dead. For Paul only those who participate in Christ's death will participate in a resurrection like his.

Telling the Corinthians about the great affliction he had recently experienced in Asia, Paul confesses that at one point he despaired for his life, thinking death was imminent. Reflecting on this experience, he writes: "We had in ourselves a death sentence, in order to rely not on ourselves but on the God who raises the dead, who has liberated us and liberates us, and who we hope will liberate us from greatest death" (2 Cor. 1:9 – 10, my translation). Whether his despair was caused by a physical illness or by being persecuted by others he does not reveal. His reference to fighting with beasts at Ephesus (1 Cor. 15:32) makes the later more likely. Though we lack the details of his tribulation, it is clear that Paul hopes that "the God who raises the dead," and who delivered him from biological death in Asia, will liberate him eventually not just from biological death. He hopes that God will also liberate him from eschatological death, the "greatest death."

Very early, Christians distinguished between biological and eschatological death, just as they made the same distinction about life. There is life in the flesh, there is life in the Spirit, and Christians may live both at the same time. There is death in nature, and there is death in sin, and unbelievers experience both at the same time. The resurrection from biological death of those in Christ is to eschatological full life. It is during their lifetime that Christians, who are not under the law, are liberated from eschatological death, the death demanded by the law. Unbelievers are buried to eschatological death. Those who live in Christ are buried to biological death. Their resurrection is the ultimate glorification of those who have been "changed into his likeness from one degree of glory to another" (2 Cor. 3:18). Now their "lowly body" is "changed to be like his glorious body by the power which enables him to subject all things to himself" (Phil. 3:21). Unlike John the Theologian in *Revelation,* Paul does not envision a resurrection of sinners. Neither does he envision the ultimate destruction of all sinners and of the rulers of the spheres in a lake of fire. Those who die in sin are left there, and the rulers of the spheres who are immortal are put under subjection. Ultimately, the God of Paul is not a God of vengeance.

As the work of God, the *Parousia* is also associated with the wrath of God. Paul understands that the ungodly and the wicked reveal the wrath of the God who abandons them to their evil devices (Rom. 1:18 – 32). He writes, "for those who are factious and do not obey the truth, but obey wickedness, there will be wrath and fury" (Rom. 2:5). The wicked who refuse to acknowledge God, he says, are "vessels of wrath" (Rom. 9:22). The wrath of God which is already operative in the life of the wicked may be administered by a "governing authority," an agent of the state who is a "servant of God to execute his wrath on the wrongdoer" (Rom. 13:4). Still, besides the manifestations of God's wrath, as he "gives up" on those who deny his divinity and power, there is also going to be "the day of wrath when God's righteous judgment will be revealed" (Rom. 2:5). Thus, those who live in Christ have been "saved by him from the wrath of God" (Rom. 5:9). During their lifetime Christians are delivered "from the wrath to come" (1 Th. 1:10), because "God has not destined us for wrath, but to obtain salvation through our Lord Jesus Christ" (1 Th. 5:9). The *Parousia* is both the day of wrath for the wicked, and the day when those who live in Christ are saved from the ultimate wrath of God by their participation in the resurrection of the dead. Exactly what the wrath of God will do on that day Paul does not say.

Paul links the *Parousia* also to a universal judgment, but the connection is not explicit. His references to it lack a time frame. He writes that "we shall all stand before the judgment seat of God" (Rom. 14:10), but also "we must all appear before the judgment seat of Christ, so that each one may receive good of evil, according to what he has done in the body" (2 Cor. 5:10). To any Jew who thinks to have an advantage over the Gentiles, and judges them to be sinners, Paul asks, "Do you suppose, O man, that when you judge those who do such things and yet do them yourself, you will escape the judgment of God?" (Rom. 2:3). In reference to the judgment Paul writes, "God shows no partiality" (Rom. 2:11). That there is going to be a righteous judgment when God, or Christ, sits on the judgment seat and some receive good and others receive evil is an indispensable part of Paul's apocalyptic vision. However, he does not expand on this motif. Following the Wisdom tradition he exclaims, "How unsearchable are his judgments!" (Rom. 11:33).

Comforting the Thessalonians who mourn the unexpected death of some members of the congregation, Paul gives a very short description of the transformation to take place at the *Parousia* of the Lord. It is clear that the death of fellow members was unexpected because Paul had made it clear that "the appointed time has grown very short." His words of consolation leave no doubt that he expects to be alive for the event. To give his words even more authority, he reveals that what he is passing on to them is "the word of the Lord." We cannot know whether these words came to Paul through the oral tradition, which is more likely, or came to him as a personal revelation. "For since we believe that Jesus died and rose again, even so, through Jesus, God will bring with him those who have fallen asleep. For this we declare to you by the word of the Lord, that we who are alive, who are left until the coming of the Lord, shall not precede those who have fallen asleep. For the Lord himself will descend from heaven with a cry of command, with the archangel's call, and with the sound of the trumpet of God. And the dead in Christ will rise first; then we who are alive, who are left, shall be caught up together with them in the clouds to meet the Lord in the air; and so we shall always be with the Lord" (1 Th. 4:14 – 17). This very personal description, in which Paul identifies himself with the Thessalonian mourners, emphasizes that those who are alive at the coming of the Lord do not have an advantage over those who have fallen asleep. Most significant is Paul's concluding observation. It defines the purpose of the coming of the Lord as well as life in the heavenly commonwealth: "and so we shall always be with the Lord." The objective is sociological, to live with the Lord.

The apocalyptic view has been characterized as escapist, as representing a way out of the harshness of life in this world. Some people think that Paul places so much value on life in heaven that life on earth loses all significance. They accuse Paul of being an other-worldly mystic dreamer. We might well ask those making such an accusation if they really think that Paul passed through life, traveling extensively in the culturally charged Roman Empire, *as though* he had not been anywhere? Do his letters give the impression that he lived in a portable Christian ghetto? Paul lived intensely in the world of human beings while waiting for the *Parousia*. Paul thought that "the appointed time is grown very short" and that "the form of this world is passing away" (1 Cor. 7:29, 31). Thus, Christians are not primarily concerned with earthly things but concerned with what is to come from heaven, their Savior, the Lord Jesus Christ (Phil. 3:20). Even as they live looking for what is to come, however, they live in the real world as citizens of the secular "conversation" (Phil. 1:27, *politeuo* comes from the root *politeia*, the assembly of voting citizens who are concerned with the welfare of the city).

We should keep in mind that for most people of the first century "this world" did not mean just the natural world, as is normal for us in the twenty first century. For them this world includes the supernatural powers designated as angels, thrones, dominions, star spirits, rulers of the world, and the cosmic spheres controlled by these powers. Paul himself reports to have been in the third heaven (2 Cor. 12:2), and it is clear that he never doubted the existence of powers in opposition to God who were quite active in human affairs. Middle Platonism in the first century and Neo-Platonism later, under the influence of Stoicism, worked out ways of integrating the divine and the human into a coherent universal structure. Thus, even in the philosophical milieu of his time, Paul did not face a choice between "this" and "another" world.

Besides, apocalypticism, whether Jewish or Christian, did not represent a unified world view. As a religious outlook, apocalypticism crossed many frontiers and offered many options. There are obvious differences, for example, between the apocalyptic descriptions we see in Paul's letters and those found in *Revelation*. As noticed earlier, Paul does not include sinners among those who are raised from the dead. He says that the Day of the Lord comes when Christ has subjugated all the powers of darkness, rather than envisioning, as in *Revelation,* that Satan and all evil doers will be destroyed after the millennium. Paul does not envision the kingdom of God established in a New Jerusalem in the midst of a still preserved Garden of Eden. When Paul says that those given spiritual bodies meet the Lord "in the air," is that the earthly atmosphere, or the third, the seventh, or the thirty third heaven? The important thing is that they shall be always with the Lord. In other words, for him it is not a matter of cosmology but of sociology.

The goal of a Christian life is not another world, but existence together with the Lord. Life together with the Lord begins here on earth for members of the body of Christ and is crowned with the reception of a spirit body that gives to life with the Lord new possibilities for relating to others. This is what God has been "about" all along and will ultimately accomplish to reveal his righteousness. The contrast is not between two different worlds but two forms of existence: life in the flesh and life in the Spirit. The goal is life in the spirit body with all the different relationships which this body makes available. Christians do not live waiting for the destruction of this world; they live waiting for the Day of the Lord when their bodies will be "like his glorious body." Christian hope is for a different way in which human beings relate to each other. That is what Paul envisions as the full effect of the power of the Gospel.

The apostle's hope for a life where "what is mortal" has been "swallowed up by life" (2 Cor. 5:4) is not a palliative administered to his converts to help them endure the hardships of economic and social injustices within the Roman Empire. He was not a "false merchant of the word of God" (2 Cor. 2:17). The hope of sharing in the glory of God, of being changed from the image of the earthly to the image of the heavenly being (1 Cor. 15:49), is not a blind hope that God will eventually do something for humankind. The assurance that God's purpose for creation will come to pass is based on three things that God has already accomplished: first, that God created the world in the first place (2 Cor. 4:4 – 6); second, that even though the visible, material structure of the present age has not changed, the cross and the resurrection of Christ have accomplished a new creation, the world of the Spirit (2 Cor. 4:18); and third, that those who have been called by God to his new creation have received the Spirit as a down payment that guarantees the full accomplishment of Gods righteousness (2 Cor. 5:5) at the day of Christ (Phil. 1:10).

Waiting for the *Parousia*, Christians live in hope strengthened by the Spirit (Rom. 8:26), walking by faith and not by sight (2 Cor. 5:7). As Paul argues, *de minoris ad maiorem*, if one grants the reality of the fallen creation in which one now lives *how much more* must one acknowledge the reality of God's power to give eternal life to those who live in the Risen Christ (Rom. 5:17). Already in antiquity, the prophets of Israel envisioned the Day of the Lord as the day in history when God would intervene to establish justice and peace among the nations. Paul envisions the Day of Christ as the day in which Christians will finally attain to full maturity in the Spirit and live together with the Lord.

XVII

When I Am Weak, Then I Am Strong

As far as Paul was concerned, his commission as an apostle did not come from any man in authority, certainly not the pillars of the Christian movement in Jerusalem. He had received his commission directly from Jesus Christ himself (Gal. 1:12). Human intermediaries would not have established his apostleship more firmly. They would have made it derivative, second-hand. Throughout his ministry Paul met the opposition of those who questioned his claim to be an apostle. Obviously, he was not one of the twelve disciples who received his commissioning from Jesus. Other apostles came to the churches established by Paul with letters signed by one of the original disciples of Jesus confirming their authorization to preach (2 Cor. 3:1 – 2). Paul felt strongly he did not need such letters. He had better evidence supporting his claim to be an apostle. The authenticity of his commissioning as an apostle was substantiated by the demonstrations of the work of the Spirit in his ministry (2 Cor. 3:3 – 4; 10:8; 11). He writes, "The signs of a true apostle were performed among you in all patience, with signs and wonders and mighty works" (2 Cor. 12:12). In Paul's estimation the proof of his apostleship was not to be found in him, but in his converts. He tells the Corinthians: "You are the seal of my apostleship in the Lord" (1 Cor. 9:1).

He had worked as an official of the Sanhedrin when he was engaged in persecuting those who proclaimed the Crucified Jesus as the Messiah. When confronted with the Risen Christ he did not change his religion, inasmuch as he continued to worship the same God he had worshipped at the Jerusalem temple. He changed his commissioning. He ceased being an agent of the Sanhedrin and became an agent of Jesus Christ. The experience on the road to Damascus did not cause him to replace official letters of the High Priest with official letters signed by the leaders of the Christian movement in Jerusalem. Paul indefatigably defended both the validity of his mission and his independence from the Jerusalem apostles because the Spirit had confirmed his ministry by the reception of the Spirit on the part of the new followers of Christ who heard him preach.

Paul's account of the incident that took place at the table fellowship of the Christian community in Antioch (Gal. 2:11 – 14) reveals that he did not consider the Jerusalem apostles his superiors. In order to know exactly what transpired at Antioch we would need Peter's version of the incident. Paul's version tells us that Paul did not think very highly of James, the one who sent investigators to Antioch, or of Peter and his double face as regards eating with Gentiles. Paul establishes the context for his forceful reaction to Peter by relating what happened when he had met with the pillars of the Christian movement in Jerusalem some time before. He reports having gone to Jerusalem with Barnabas and Titus "by revelation" (Gal. 2:2). He went to meet privately with the apostles and tell them the Gospel he had been preaching during the previous seventeen years. The meeting ended, Paul says, with "those who were reputed to be something (what they were makes no difference to me; God shows no partiality) — those, I say, who were of repute added nothing to me; . . . and when they perceived the grace that was given to me, James and Cephas and John, who were reputed to be pillars, gave to me and Barnabas the right hand of fellowship" (Gal. 2:6, 9).

Paul also reports that at that time he strongly resisted efforts made by some who spied on Titus, a Gentile, and were eager to have him circumcised. He says that his determination to prevent the circumcision of Titus was his way of preserving "the truth of the Gospel" (Gal. 2:5). Of course, the truth of the Gospel does not consist of the notion that Gentiles need not be circumcised as were proselytes to Judaism. It is, rather, the affirmation that those who are in Chris are distinguished by the gift of the Spirit, not by circumcision. After the resurrection of Christ the barriers that had been used to make distinctions among humans had become irrelevant. "There is neither Jew nor Greek, there is neither slave nor free, there is neither male nor female, for you are all one in Christ Jesus" (Gal. 3:28). Paul is not impressed by the reputations of the pillars of the Christian movement in Jerusalem and by taking away the ranking of Jews, free people and males as above Greeks, slaves and females, Paul shows himself working toward a different kind of human community ruled by the dictum "God shows no partiality."

Paul was not at odds with the Jerusalem community and its leaders. He went to see James, Peter and John at Jerusalem to coordinate his activities with theirs, and he reports that his objective was accomplished at their meeting (Gal. 2:8 – 9). He admits that the only commitment he made to them was to "remember the poor," and he did take that commitment seriously (Gal. 2:10). In *To the Corinthians II* we may have two notes sent separately by Paul to the Corinthians asking them to set aside money for the poor in Jerusalem before his arrival (chapters 8 and 9). In *To the Romans* he writes from Corinth saying that he would like to visit the Roman Christians and have them send him on to Spain. This wish, however, has to be postponed because he must take the money he has collected in Macedonia and Achaia (Greece) for the poor in Jerusalem (Rom. 15:26). There is no doubt that Paul saw himself as a Christian who was loyal to and a servant of all other Christians, but no other Christian had authority over him.

The only authority Paul would recognize is the authority of the Spirit that activates all the ministrations accomplished by women and men who are guided by the Spirit and empowered by the love of God. This means that the unity of the various Christian congregations that are emerging throughout the Roman Empire is not the result of the leadership of the Jerusalem apostles, their administrative decisions, their successful efforts to maintain acceptable creedal formulas, or their ability to have good relations with the governing authorities. Rather, it is the natural outcome of the unity of the Spirit, who is constantly working toward the building up of the church (1 Cor. 14:12).

Appealing to the Philippians to be of one mind and to let that one mind be the mind of Christ, Paul bases his entreaty on their participation in the Spirit, their incentives of love, and their encouragement in Christ (Phil. 2:1). These three things are what unify the Christian communities located in cities scattered all over the Roman world. Christian unity is not some monumental idea to be expressed dogmatically or some ecclesiastical organization to be achieved politically. Effective Christian unity in concrete communities of people is the work of the Spirit that provides the encouragements in Christ that work themselves out as acts of love. That is the way in which Paul views the Christian movement. All Christian men and women are members of the body of Christ. As such they are the means by which the Risen Lord is present and active in the world liberating and giving life to those who live under the power of sin and death. At the time of Paul, the Christian movement had not yet become an institution with officials and authorized channels through which power should flow. Institutions adopt structures available in the culture where they are to operate. Inevitably, they develop cultural patterns of their own and become part of the cultural mix in which they find themselves. As a man in Christ, Paul did not see himself as a member of an institution, but as a member of the body of Christ, where there are no secondary authorities. Those working in Christian institutions at times find themselves wondering whether they are working for Christ or for "the Church." Paul never faced this problem.

Paul insisted on the equality of all Christians. To the Corinthians who were choosing their favorite apostle and pledging allegiance to him, thereby breaking the unity of the Spirit, Paul asks the rhetorical question, "Is Christ divided? Was Paul crucified for you?" (1 Cor. 1:13). No apostle could possibly be the one on whom other Christians depended for life and freedom. All apostles could only be servants of Christ and, like Paul, "in debt" to preach the

Meditations on the Letters of Paul

Gospel to all women and men. For those apostles who make claims to privileges, like deserving to be paid for their service, Paul has very harsh words. He would never burden anyone with payment. "What I do I will continue to do, in order to undermine the claim of those who would like to claim that in their boasted mission they work on the same terms as we do. For such men are false apostles, deceitful workmen, disguising themselves as apostles of Christ. And no wonder, for even Satan disguises himself as an angel of light. So it is not strange if his servants also disguise themselves as servants of righteousness. Their end will correspond to their deeds" (2 Cor. 11:12 – 15). His mission for Christ is a service, not a job.

Even though it is not unusual to think of Paul as the lone traveler along the excellent Roman highways, his missionary activity was not a private affair. As in the words just quoted, he regularly says "we," referring to the team of which he was a member. Among his associates, Sosthenes, Silvanus, and Timothy are named as co-authors of some of his letters (1 Cor. 1:1; 2 Cor. 1:1; 1 Th. 1:1; Phil. 1:1), and he credits Silvanus and Timothy with having shared in the preaching of the Gospel at Corinth (2 Cor. 1:19). At the time of the Corinthian correspondence, Titus, his "partner and fellow-worker" (2 Cor. 8:6, 23; 12:18), was Paul's intermediary (2 Cor. 2:13; 8:16) while Apollos, whom Paul had urged to visit Corinth, preferred to stay away as long as the situation there remained unsettled (1 Cor. 16:12). Of all his fellow-workers, he had the most intimate sentiments for Timothy. Paul wrote of him, "I have no one like him, who will be genuinely anxious for your welfare. They all look after their own interests, not those of Jesus Christ. But Timothy's worth you know, how as a son with a father he has served me in the gospel" (Phil. 2:20 – 22). Others designated as fellow-workers are Urbanus (Rom. 16:9), Philemon (Philem. 1), Mark, Aristarchus, Demas and Luke (Philem. 23).

Attention must be given to the way in which Paul refers to the activities of women as apostles and fellow-workers. There are two husband and wife teams singled out by Paul. Priscilla and Aquila form one (Rom. 16:3; 1 Cor. 16:19), and Andronichus and Junias the other (Rom. 16:7). Notable about the former is that Priscilla is mentioned first — apparently she was the leader of the team. About the second couple Paul makes several comments. He points out that they are fellow-Jews, fellow-prisoners, well respected as apostles and that they became Christians before him. He also mentions Tryphaena and Tryphosa who, given the commonality of their names we may assume to be sisters. They are "workers in the Lord." The beloved Persis distinguishes herself for having "worked hard in the Lord" (Rom. 16:12), and Mary "has worked hard" at the Christian community at Rome (Rom. 16:6). Paul's high esteem of Chloe, who has agents traveling around the empire (1 Cor. 1:11), Phoebe, a deacon [minister] of the church at Cenchreae (Rom. 16:1), and of Tryphaena, Tryphosa, Persis, Mary, Priscilla and Junias gives ample evidence of the full participation of women as co-workers in the proclamation of the Gospel in the areas where Paul worked.

That Paul defended the equality of men and women is also in evidence in what he says concerning marital relationships. "The husband should give to his wife her conjugal rights, and likewise the wife to her husband. For the wife does not rule over her own body, but the husband does; likewise the husband does not rule over his own body, but the wife does" (1 Cor. 7:3 – 4). There can be no doubt that this statement must have been quite controversial within the Jewish context of early Christianity. Contrary to what is usually said about Paul's views of women by ascribing to him letters written pseudonymously thirty years after his death, he elevated the status of women both in the bedroom and in the homes where Christians met to break bread together with their Lord. When the Christian movement became an ecclesiastical institution and an official clergy became dominated by men, they eventually barred women from leadership in the church. That had not been the case at all at the beginning. As testified by the gospel *According to John*, in movements at the Christian periphery women continued to be prominent leaders well into the second century, just as they had been at Paul's times.

Meditations on the Letters of Paul

As it reads now, *To the Corinthians I* has two interpolations which try to make Paul agree with later developments as the Christian movement became an institution and worked toward the exclusion of women from active participation, or leadership, in the worship services at the churches. The first, found in 1 Corinthians 11:2 – 16, has a convoluted exposition of the subservient position of women but admits that women can pray and prophesy in church, with one proviso. While men must do it with their heads uncovered, women doing it must have their heads covered. This section was apparently further touched by another hand to say that while the subservient position of women may obtain in society this is not the case among Christians. "Nevertheless, in the Lord woman is not independent of man nor man of woman; for as woman was made from man, so man is now born of woman. And all things are from God" (1 Cor. 11:11 – 12). This establishes reciprocity between the sexes, rather than the superiority of males, contradicting the hierarchical description of verse 3.

The second interpolation, found in 1 Corinthians 13:33b – 36, is an echo of 1 Timothy 2:8 – 15. It imposes total silence on the part of women at church. Paul's high regard for the women who lead churches and collaborate with him cannot be correlated to this point of view. Even the second hand in the first interpolation does not agree to this extreme position; it allows women to pray and prophesy at the churches. If one reads *To the Corinthians I* skipping over these interpolations, Paul's line of reasoning flows quite smoothly without interruptions. Both interpolations claim that what they teach obtains in "all the churches" (1 Cor. 11:16; 13:33b). I find it hard to believe that Paul would claim to be the spokesman for "all the churches of the saints" because he insists that he is not a church official in authority. That could only be claimed by one who was involved in the institutionalization of the church toward the end of the first century.

The establishment of uniformity under ecclesiastical authority is not what Paul was about. Because of the full participation of women as coworkers in his mission work, in the second century the Ebionites accused him of having had unseemly relations with women. *The Acts of Paul and Thecla*, a second century romantic legend, was published to argue against this scurrilous attacks. It also presented Paul as a model of virginity and celibacy, and as one who defended the right of women to preach and to baptize. It is now understood that this work was a section of a larger work known as *The Acts of Paul*. As a separate pamphlet, *The Acts of Paul and Thecla* enjoyed wide circulation not only in Greek but also in Syriac, Latin, Armenian, Coptic and Ethiopic translations. The popularity of *The Acts of Paul and Thecla* tells us that the marginalization of women from the Christian ministry that began at the end of the first century met with persistent resistance for some time.

Paul's apostolic mission was challenged primarily in Thessalonica, Corinth and Galatia. To defend his apostleship to the Corinthians, Paul resorts "to boast[ing] in his weakness," even if doing it was not "according to the Lord." It may be, however, that Paul is being ironic, putting things upside down. The Corinthians accused Paul of being meek and humble when among them, but sending them bold and threatening letters when away (2 Cor. 10:1, 10); he likes to impose himself on others, while claiming to be subject to Christ (2 Cor. 10:7, 8); compared to other legitimate apostles, he is a nobody (2 Cor. 10:12; 12:11); his efforts to guide the spiritual life of the Corinthians are overreaching because his territory does not include Europe (2 Cor. 10:4); he shows his disregard for the Corinthians by not accepting financial help from them, even though he has accepted it from others (2 Cor. 11:9, 11, 16); by employing himself as an artisan, he makes a fool of himself and embarrasses the Corinthians (2 Cor. 11:7, 8); the only explanation for his success in converting them to his version of the Gospel is that he used underhanded ways; he got the better of them by guile (2 Cor. 12:16).

The manner in which Paul makes reference to all these charges has an ironic tone. If the charges were true, Paul would have been conducting himself "according to the flesh," and that is the one thing that Paul most strenuously tried to avoid. According to him, as already noted, the proof of his apostleship is none other than the conversion of the Corinthians themselves. To defend himself he does not direct their attention to himself but to them: "You are the seal of my apostleship in the Lord" (1 Cor. 9:1).

The Galatians disqualified Paul for lack of proper credentials. He was not one of the original twelve. As a second stringer he was only trying to please those who had taught him the Gospel. To the Galatians Paul insists on the divine origin of his call and of his Gospel. He is not an apostle "from men nor through man, but through Jesus Christ and God the Father who raised him from the dead" (Gal. 1:1). What he preached was not what somebody taught him but what came to him "through a revelation of Jesus Christ" (Gal. 1:12). As a matter of fact, he had not been taught by the Christian leaders in Jerusalem. He had not spent enough time with them for that to have happened. During his first seventeen years as a Christian, he had spent only fifteen days in Jerusalem with Peter and James (Gal. 1:18; 2:1).Paul answered the charges made by the Galatians with a contrary to fact conditional sentence and a rhetorical question. "If I were still pleasing men, I should not be a slave of Christ" (Gal. 1:10), and "If I . . . still preach circumcision, why am I still persecuted?" (Gal. 5:11). As a matter of fact, he is a slave of Christ; therefore, he is still being persecuted because he has not been working to please men, and he has not given in to the pressure of Jewish Christians who wish to keep Christianity a Jewish sect.

The Thessalonians seem to have understood Paul's Gospel as a license to libertinism. In this they were similar to the Corinthians. Paul defends himself writing, "For our appeal does not spring from error or uncleanness, nor is it made with guile; but just as we have been approved by God to be entrusted with the gospel, so we speak, not to please men, but to please God who tests our hearts. For we never used either words of flattery, as you know, or a cloak for greed, as God is witness, nor did we seek glory from men, whether from you or from others, though we might have made demands as apostles of Christ" (1 Th. 2:3 – 6). These words can only be understood to detail charges of preaching a spurious gospel that condones uncleanness and of having used guile and flattery to take money from them. Paul reminds them that his team worked "night and day, that we might not burden any of you" (1 Th. 2:9), and then repeats the instructions he gave them concerning sexual passions (1 Th. 4:2 – 7). These end with the words, "For God has not called us for uncleanness, but in holiness." The radical nature of Paul's Gospel, it seems, has been difficult to understand from the beginning.

Paul never ceases to give credit to God for what is happening among human beings on account of the New Creation brought about by the resurrection of Christ. As he writes to the Corinthians, "He is the source of your life in Christ Jesus" (1 Cor. 1:30). He also credits God for giving him a "thorn in the flesh." To his repeated pleas to be relieved from it, he received the oracular answer "My grace is sufficient for you, for my power is made perfect in weakness" (2 Cor. 12:9). Does this mean that unless there is weakness God's power may not be fully perceived? Or, does it mean that unless there is weakness God's power may not be active? Are weakness and power related in the order of knowledge, or on the order of reality? Is Paul setting forth a general principle that is true in the lives of all Christians who serve Christ while waiting for the *Parousia*? Or, is Paul speaking autobiographically?

From the context it is clear that Paul saw his own weakness as participation in the weakness of Christ (2 Cor. 13:4). He was "always being given up to death for Jesus' sake" (2 Cor. 4:11). The notion that trials, misfortunes, sickness, etc., are already forms of death, or at least a diminishment of life, is well known in the Old Testament. Sickness, poverty, or social and political powerlessness are the result either of the arm of Sheol reaching out to embrace and swallow its victims or of God dragging one to the very gates of Sheol. On the other hand, health, wealth, and general prosperity reflect a positive connection with the living God.

Paul understood his weakness, however, not in connection with the power of Sheol, but in connection with the cross of Christ. For him, weakness was essential to his Christology. He was weak because he participated, while serving his Lord, in his Lord's cross (Gal. 4:14). His service was patterned after that of Christ. His apostleship, like Christ's sojourn on earth, was characterized by his refusal to claim the perquisites that normally would have been considered his (1 Cor. 9:1 – 18). If he says, "Be imitators of me," it is in reference to this attitude of his. That is why he adds "as I am of Christ" (1 Cor. 11:1). He wishes that all Christians would adopt this posture in life, which is powerfully described in the Christ hymn he quotes in *To the Philippians* (2:6 – 11). The perfection of power in weakness may be understood only in terms of the perfection of the cross at Easter (2 Cor. 13:4).

Psychological explanations of the weakness of Christians, or moral lessons derived from it, are a caricature of what Paul is concerned with. The manifestation of power in weakness is neither a ploy to teach moral lessons nor a necessity for humans to realize their impotence before the burden of sin. Paul is talking about the agents of God who extend the benefits of salvation to humankind, not in a triumphalist manner but as slaves. The cross they carry is the cross of their Lord, but they carry it in their own society and in their own culture as their own cross. If the cross reveals them as weak, it is in the process by which God's power is bringing to light that which is not.

The relation of weakness to power is built into the very structure of the New Creation. God's power is manifest only in those who recognize themselves as his slaves and, therefore, claim nothing for themselves. The servants of the Lord undergo the trials and tribulations that life in the flesh inevitably makes them face in full confidence of what the Lord has already accomplished. They are neither rooted in the ways in which their cultures operate nor are they supported by trust in the flesh. The power of God is what upholds their lives and gives them strength. With Paul they confess, "When I am weak, then I am strong" (2 Cor. 12:10). That is so because for Paul the crucifixion and the resurrection of Christ cannot be considered separate events. Together they constitute the standard of the Christian life.

Epilogue

All biblical authors wrote under inspiration, but their writings reveal significant differences in their personalities, their vocabularies, their worlds of meaning, etc. Their theologies reflect their cultures, and they must be judged in terms of them. What strikes readers of Paul are his deep roots in Judaism and his independence and creativity in the culturally charged Roman empire. He traveled a lonely path in the footsteps of the Christ with whom he had chosen to be crucified so as to live in a new creation. He was not a recognized leader of the Christian movement during his lifetime, and his interpretation of the significance of the cross and the resurrection of Christ was not accepted by the contemporary leaders of Christianity and has not been the prevailing way of understanding them throughout Christian history. His claim that the resurrection of Christ was the creation of a new Adam, and that all human beings are invited to become creatures of the new creation, constituted a bold theological opening of the gates to life, as well as a radical departure from an ethnic definition of the people of God. This redefinition of the elect did not appeal to most followers of Jesus, and was easily misinterpreted by many who heard Paul preach.

Paul's first basic insight was that the cross of Jesus and the resurrection of Christ Jesus meant the end of the hegemony of sin and of the law that serves to define it. His second insight was that the creation of new life in the Risen Lord offers possibilities totally different from the ones offered by views of the cross as a sacrifice, a ransom, or a model. Paul does not preach a substitutionary atonement, or righteousness by a legal sleight of hand. Paul's Gospel does not say that the law demands the death of sinners and that since Christ died for them they need not die. His Gospel says that sinners must crucify themselves with Christ and thereby become free from the law because its jurisdiction is limited to the fallen creation. Those who live in the new creation are free from its power to condemn. They live in newness of life by the power that raised Christ from the dead. Paul's Gospel proclaims freedom from the law, sin and death because God demonstrated an amazing love for sinners when Christ died to put an end to the overwhelming power of sin. Paul's Gospel announces God's righteous call to have faith in God's action in Christ and participate in crucifixion and resurrection. The call of God is to leave behind the life lived in the flesh and according to the flesh, whether outside the law or under the law, and live empowered by the Spirit who raised Christ from the dead. His is not a Gospel that trades on guilt, frustration or fear. His is the Gospel of new life in the Spirit, enjoyed by members of the body of Christ who live in a manner that is worthy of the Lord they serve.

Paul recognizes that those who live in Christ by the power and the guidance of the Spirit still live in the flesh, that is, in the natural environment of human society where the power of the law, sin, and death still holds sway. In this condition, Christians live in tension between the desires of the flesh and the will to live according to the dictates of the mind renewed by the Spirit that is convicted as to what is the will of God. Christians live in the flesh and in the Spirit, crucified with Christ so as to live by the power of the new creation, free from the law, sin, and death but slaves of Christ for the sake of their neighbors. This tension is difficult to sustain and often is resolved in favor of one or the other. The history of Christianity may be written in terms of periods when Christians have lived under the burden of the cross and periods when they have lived enjoying the glories of the resurrection. In our times Christians seem to be inebriated with the power of the resurrection. Pauline Christianity, however, requires keeping the cross and the resurrection in existential balance.

Christians live by faith, hope and love. They receive the energy and the motivations for living from what God did in the past in the Christ Event *and* from what God promises to do in the future Parousia when God's dominion over all creatures is restored. Then God's righteousness will ultimately be demonstrated. In the meantime, God's righteousness is demonstrated by the way in which those who live in Christ practice their faith and hope in acts of love for their neighbors.

Paul sees those who exercise faith in God's righteousness as the heirs of Abraham. Unlike the author of the *Letter of James* who considers that Abraham demonstrated his faith by his willingness to sacrifice Isaac, Paul sees Abraham's faith demonstrated by taking seriously God's promise, and starting to walk toward the promised land. Paul understood that faith in the one who promised is what makes a promise real. In other words, a promise cannot stand by itself; it stands or falls on the relationship of its recipient with the one who promised.

The author of the *Letter of James* follows what was considered central to the Rabbis of antiquity and even today is considered central by orthodox Jews and many Christians. According to this interpretation, by obeying the command to sacrifice Isaac Abraham demonstrated that an external word of authority must trump all reasoning. Abraham must have remembered God's promise that his descendants would become a great nation through Isaac. He certainly could have thought that he had had a nightmare that needed to be forgotten. He could have conceived a dozen reasons why the command to sacrifice Isaac made no sense and should not be obeyed. But Abraham did not hesitate and obeyed the voice of authority, showing that faith must trump reason.

By contrast, Paul does not see Abraham as the father of those whose faith trumps reason. He sees Abraham as the father of those who by faith crucify themselves with Christ, laying hold of the promise of life in the Spirit as new creatures. The Spirit enables them to use their minds, energizes them to reason properly, evaluate options and determine the "good and acceptable and perfect" will of God. Those accepted by God are those who practice the obedience of faith, that is, those who respond to the love of God demonstrated in the death of Christ. Their minds tell them the reasonable way to live by faith. Faith is a way of being a whole person by the power of the Spirit, not a split person who behaves unreasonably.

A common misreading of Paul makes him the originator of a private religion, transforming the ethnic religion of a group of tribes into an individualistic one. In this view, Judaism suffered from the contradiction of worshipping the God of the universe who had no rivals while claiming that God was concerned only with a chosen ethnic group. Paul, it is said, broke down the ethnic exclusivism of Judaism and offered the universal God of Judaism to all humanity on an individual basis. It is quite true that Paul makes the salvation offered by God to the Israelites available to all humanity, but not on an individual basis. He broke down barriers, as I have been emphasizing. This interpretation of Paul, however, overlooks that Paul did not dismiss Torah's doctrine of election, but re-interpreted it. Election is still operative. The Risen Christ is the seed of Abraham to whom the promise was made. All those who participate in his death and resurrection, both Jews and Gentiles are elected in him. Paul re-interprets who are the elect not as individuals, but as the body of the Risen Christ. Christ is present in the world not in individual members but in the Christian community.

Those who are buried and raised with Christ individually at baptism are incorporated into the body of Christ. Paul does not teach a substitutionary atonement to be applied individually to those who prove themselves worthy; rather he teaches that Christ died once for all, not privately for each individual. Paul teaches a participatory atonement where those who believe God die and are raised with Christ. Those who are baptized put away the "old person" and become a "new person" as they are integrated into the "new creation." They do not thereby become new individuals, but they become members of the body of Christ. The Christian life, according to Paul, is not to be lived privately but in community. As members of the body of Christ, creatures of the new creation, Christians make the Risen Christ present in human history. It is in the community of believers that the mind of Christ is at work and it is as a community that Christians are the temple of the Holy Spirit, the tangible mock-up of the cosmic reality of the new creation.

Besides, the metaphor "the body of Christ" makes the point that this community of the faithful is not a bureaucratic organization structured hierarchically, but a living organism structured organically. The members have been given discreet talents in order to perform specific tasks within the body. The differentiation of gifts among the members of the body does not set up some above others. In Christ all are equally important for the health of the organism. The body of Christ directed by the mind of Christ is characterized by the diversity of its members and the organic unity that gives it vitality and effectiveness.

Paul understands that those who join Christ in his death in order to participate in his resurrection do not achieve their goal immediately. Faith in God's action in Christ places Christians on a field in which they must grow in faith. Salvation by the grace of God does not mean that those who have found grace have nothing else to do, other than to have faith in God. For Paul, Christians must live out their faith as obedience, and obedience to the will of God as determined by the renewed mind must be demonstrated in a manner of living that is worthy of the Lord. The life of faith is a constant progression from glory to glory as faith responds to the call of God and pushes on toward the goal of eventual full glorification at the *Parousia*. Paul envisions the Christian life as a development from childhood to adulthood, a process of maturation produced by the obedience of faith. This is not just a matter of becoming mature intellectually. It is a maturation demonstrated by "walking" in the pursuit of love.

Like Plato and later the Stoics, but unlike Aristotle, Paul saw the universe as one entity. It is, therefore, possible to see in the natural world the power and the glory of God. For Paul both nature and history reveal the mind of God. Thus, while God's being is inscrutable and God's ways are beyond human understanding, what happens in the world, both in the lives of human beings and in the rest of creation, is according to the will of God, except when God "gives up" on those who do evil. In other words, Paul views nature as demonstrating the mind of God. There is, therefore, some correspondence between living according to the will of God and living according to nature. There must be concord between the mind of God revealed in nature and in Christ and the mind of Christians who live in Christ by the power of the Spirit. Having the mind of Christ, the Christian community re-enacts the trajectory of Christ's life cycle. The mind of Christ is not unreasonable. Reason is one of the natural endowments God has given to all human beings so that the Holy Spirit who renews and energizes reason does not function as a superior authority with veto power. The Holy Spirit and human reason work together within God's creation.

For Paul a gospel that is not liberating is no Gospel. His insistence on the freedom for which Christ has made women and men free is to be understood as the freedom of creatures living constrained by the love of God. The freedom of Christians is not a natural endowment, but a corollary of life in the Spirit: "where the Spirit of the Lord is, there is freedom." It is not for creatures to enjoy autonomous, absolute freedom. God is the one who has control of the frontier between the things that are and the things that are not, the realm of actuality and the realm of potentiality. God is the only one who is absolutely free. Humans may be free only in relation to what already is. Freedom depends on power; it is as strong or as weak as the power that sustains it. Almighty God has absolute freedom. Christians are free from the power of the law to condemn sin; they are free from death, not by their own power, but because they are in Christ, the one who destroyed the power of sin and triumphed over death.

Paul's Gospel proclaimed the righteousness of God demonstrated in the death and the resurrection of Christ. He concluded that from that moment forward the heirs of the promise to Abraham were no longer the Jews as such, but all those who die and are raised with Christ no matter their ethnic, economic of gender status. As Paul says, "There is neither Jew nor Greek, there is neither slave nor free, there is neither male nor female; for you are all one in Christ Jesus." Thus, Paul's Gospel was an agent for the elimination of barriers, frontiers, and divisions within humanity. Among humans, it is common to establish differentiations giving preferences and privileges that bestow higher status on some to the detriment of others. It has been observed often that for human beings death is the great equalizer; Paul sees the cross of Christ as the great equalizer. The Gospel establishes that God has no favorites. God is impartial. In Christ, no matter where in the human scale one may be found, all are equal; all are "saints." Because his Gospel disallowed the markers that establish ethnic, economic and gender inequalities, Paul found himself persecuted by those who wished to uphold their privileged status. As a Jew, a scion of the slave owning class and a male he had undoubtedly enjoyed the privileges of his economic, social and gender status, but Paul confesses that he came to consider all natural or culturally established privileges as refuse ("dung" in the KJV).

In view of all these aspects of the Gospel proclaimed by Paul, one cannot but find helpful insights in his vision of God's righteousness. This does not mean that one cannot also find some of his premises problematic. Paul's Gospel is that God is at work in the world in order to fulfill the purpose of creation. The way he conceived of God's activity, both in nature and in Christ, was dependent on the views of the structure of nature and the theological parameters available to him at the time. To take Paul seriously does not require acceptance of his cosmology or the setting up of dogmas based on his metaphors. To admire his theological vision is not necessary to become bound by his symbolic universe. His vision of the righteousness of God expressed within his apocalyptic worldview must be read as analogical. It expresses in human terms the marvels of God's purposes. Recognizing this should tell us that we must not give ultimate significance to our own ways of expressing the action of God in the world. Faith needs to be expressed, but its expressions can only be understood within the confines of the contemporary views of reality. As I have tried to point out throughout my meditations on his letters, Paul expressed himself within a particular cultural context, and its limitations are found in his writings. His was a hierarchical and deterministic culture where manual labor was looked down upon and slavery was institutionalized. He did not feel his mission was to bring about changes in the fallen creation, but to bring about a community which lived already in the new creation. Living in a totally different culture now, it is up to us to determine the will of God for our own times.

Paul's theological groundbreaking is a model to be imitated. As already said, Paul's Gospel is a Gospel that breaks the barriers that separate humans. He identified ethnic (Jew/Greek), economic (slave/free) and natural (male/female) barriers. Would it not be an extension of his legacy to claim that the Gospel should also break religious barriers that have had a nefarious effect in the history of humanity? A Christianity that is divided along sectarian and denominational lines is at odds with Paul's Gospel. His Gospel tells us that the righteousness of God is at work for the benefit of all human beings. Extending his universalist vision to the divisions within our world is to be alert to the power of the Gospel. The body of Christ consists of members with very different personal histories.

Paul's apocalyptic expectation that the *Parousia* would take place during his lifetime has been proven false by experience. In fact, his apocalyptic understanding of the turning of the ages, with its concept of the Fall and its inherent predestination, is difficult to defend in today's scientific symbolic universe. It is noteworthy, however, that Paul's apocalypticism is prophetic, not mythological, in as much as it does not include elements from the myths of creation that abound in the apocalyptic literature of the time. The prophets did not just *fore* tell the future. They spoke *for* God analyzing the present.

Apocalypticists read the Scriptures guided by two basic rules of interpretation: 1) all Scripture was written with "the time of the end" in view, and 2) we are living in "the time of the end." These two hermeneutical principles inform the writings of Paul, the writings of the Covenanters of Qumran, the Dead Sea Scrolls, as well as

Meditations on the Letters of Paul

all apocalypticists through time, including those of the twenty first century. Apparently, that previous claims to be living in "the end" have proven wrong is irrelevant to succeeding apocalypticists. The author of the *Second Letter of Peter*, writing at the beginning of the second century, recognized that the "delay" was a problem that gave rise to "scoffers" who asked, "Where is the promise of his coming? For ever since the fathers fell asleep, all things have continued as they were from the beginning of creation" (2 Pet. 3:4). This author has an answer for the scoffers. They fail to realize that "with the Lord one day is as a thousand years, and a thousand years as one day" (2 Pet. 3:8). His answer, however, is flawed. He failed to realize that on the basis of his argument no one can claim to be living in "the time of the end," since it is impossible for human beings to determine the time in God's clock.

The scientific world of today was made possible by the approach to nature taught in antiquity by Aristotle. He was the one who drew a line between the natural world and the gods. As already noted, Paul lived in the Hellenistic culture in which Plato and the Stoics were the major cultural forces. They did not exclude God from the natural world, and Paul proclaimed the Gospel of God's love as an active force in the world.

Our understanding of the universe and how things in nature work has been made possible by the great advances brought about by scientific methods of investigation. This places us at a great distance from the apocalyptic universe where divine forces populating the hierarchical spheres in space are also active in the human world. We find ourselves in a different symbolic universe, one in which deterministic views of the future are very problematic and the scientific understanding of celestial space has taken away notions of the chain of being; but this does not mean that we cannot understand Paul's gospel and be energized by it. Science cannot say a word about God, either in a positive or in a negative way. That we cannot find a better answer to the presence of so much evil in the world than the one provided by apocalypticism does not demand that we must either cling to an apocalyptic worldview or cease claiming that God is actively carrying out the purpose of creation in the world. It only demands that we be cognizant of our limitations and recognize ourselves as God's creatures.

To affirm that we are God's creation by the power of the Spirit, not just part of nature, can only be done by faith. Here is where Paul's Gospel connects with all times and all cultures. Faith in the power of God to bring about life by the Spirit that raised Christ from the dead is not within the competence of science. Faith is neither supported nor threatened by science. It only tells science to recognize that not all that is real is amenable to scientific scrutiny. Human faculties and experiences do not consist only of what can be observed under scientific controls. The reconstruction of the past done by history in our days is controlled by modern historical methods, but never attains to the level of certainty that the study of nature attains. In both cases, however, whatever conclusions are reached are by their very nature liable to be overturned by further investigations. We have come to realize that the scientific obsession for objectivity is a chimera. Our times may require a new interpretation of the traditional Christian meta-narrative of the activity of God in the world, but this challenge provides an opportunity for avenues of understanding; it is not an impassable barrier to the significance of the past. That is precisely what Paul did with the meta-narrative of Judaism by his conflation of apocalyptic and wisdom traditions. The Spirit that gives life in the Risen Christ can empower our minds to envision the will of God for our own time so that freedom from sin and death and freedom for God's future may remain a reality in God's world. To affirm that the Creator God is faithful to his creation is what faith in the righteousness of God does at all times.

The stories from the patriarchs and the psalms, to which Paul appeals in support of the metaphors with which he expresses his faith in the righteousness of God, are exactly that — stories and psalms with which previous believers expressed their faith in the righteousness of God. The list of those who acted by faith given by the author of *To the Hebrews* is another indication that to be a Christian is not determined by theological definitions but by what faith makes a person do. To this Paul is a most powerful witness. Paul's theological expositions are intimately linked to what his addressees were doing or about to do. Some time later, when Christianity became an institution, faith as a way of being became THE FAITH that the institution defines and its members must believe

The Gospel of Paul is the Gospel of the power that makes human beings free for God and neighbor. This Gospel is capable of being preached in any culture because it is not bound by ideological parameters or dogmatic truths. His test for truth is practical and experiential. When truth is reduced to the quality of a certain piece of information that a few claim to possess, it has in effect been made into an idol. Paul insists that truth, divine wisdom, is to be found in what God did in Christ. This means that truth is to be found in the realm of being, rather than the realm of knowledge. Writing to the Romans about their disputes concerning the proper diet, Paul relativizes the notion that some foods are clean and others are unclean. He does so by saying that this distinction can be made only in the realm of knowledge, but not in the realm of being, that is, in the reality of the created world. According to Paul, knowledge "puffs up," but love builds up. Love, however, can only be found in the realm of being. In the realm of knowledge, love lacks its essential power. The realm of knowledge operates within cultural conditions that classify beliefs and opinions. In the realm of knowledge love of neighbor may become an abstraction that is based on prejudices.

The tragic flaw of fundamentalism, no matter in which religion it is found, is that when truth and love find themselves in opposition it prescribes allegiance to propositional truths. Paul is aware of this dilemma and prescribes allegiance to love. Truth and love find themselves in opposition, however, only when truth is in the realm of knowledge, the realm privileged by fundamentalism. Paul's truth, like love, can only be found in the realm of being, the realm where creation takes place.

The question to be asked of any gospel is, "What manner of life does it promote?" Only those whose lives are enactments of the love of God energized by their faith and hope can witness to the truth of the Gospel as members of the body of Christ. For Paul, the significance of Christ is not bound to the details of his teachings or his miracles. The meaning of Christ's death is that it came about in obedience to God's purpose to put an end to sin and death. The meaning of Christ's resurrection is that it brought about a New Creation. Paul claims that he gained this vision of what Christ means by revelation. He then explicated this vision by reference to the Scriptures. Now those who believe that God's purpose is being accomplished, and determine to become agents of God's righteousness in the world by the power of the Spirit that raised Christ from the dead, have the responsibility to demonstrate God's love in the world. The Gospel is not a matter of knowledge, but of power to live. That is what Paul demanded of his converts. According to Paul, the mission of Christians is to activate the power of the Gospel among their neighbors and thus make present the Risen Christ as the giver of life.

Index of References to the Letters of Paul

To the Romans

Reference	Page
1:1	47
1:3-4	64
1:5	112, 116
1:9	19, 38
1:16	23, 155
1:18-32	179
1:20	50, 102
1:21	51
2:3	179
2:5	179
2:11	87, 101, 179
2:14-15	51, 102
2:16	19, 56
2:17-21	102
2:25	47
2:27	102
2:29	59
3:2	78
3:3	77
3:8	55
3:7	102
3:9	76, 103
3:20	75, 101, 103
3:21	113
3:27	89
3:29	55
3:31	82, 92
4:2-3	113, 114
4:6	113
4:10	113
4:13-14	44, 113
4:15	20, 45, 75, 90, 96, 101
4:16-20	45
4:17	154
4:19	150
4:21	46
5:1-5	31
5:3	159
5:5	36, 60
5:6	30
5:8	31, 143, 169
5::9	179
5:10, 15, 17	54
5:12	96, 103
5:13	104
5:14	103
5:17	103, 183
5:19	66
5:20	96, 104
6:1	55
6:2-3	131
6:4	165, 166

6:6	130	8:23-27	53
6:6-11	124	8:24	156, 173
6:12	130	8:26	183
6:15	75, 95, 103, 111	8:27	60
6:16-17	143	8:28	32
6:17	60, 145	8:29	72
6:17-18	165	8:31	55
6:20	159	8:35-39	32
7:4	106, 130, 131	9:2-4	78
7:5	103, 125, 126	9:4	150
7:6	94, 145	9:5	64, 78
7:7	55, 96	9:6-13	79
7:9	103	9:8	47
7:10	96	9:11-12	113
7:14	90, 124	9:14	80
7:19	58	9:18	80
7:21	92	9:19	55, 80
7:22	89, 92, 117	9:21-23	54, 81
7:23	145	9:22	179
7:24	130	9:31-32	112, 152
7:25	93	9:32	82
8:1	104	9:33	54
8:2	39, 89, 145	10:2	83
8:3	63, 90, 145	10:3	82
8:6	37, 39, 57	10:4	94
8:7	89	10:5	112
8:8	125	10:6-9	112
8:9	36, 38, 125	10:8	60
8:11	37, 38, 90	10:9	83, 143
8:12	127, 131	10:10	60
8:13	123	10:14	112
8:14	36	10:16	113
8:15	37	10:21	83, 112
8:16	38	11:1-2	83
8:19-23	157	11:5-6	83

11:11	84
11:12, 24	54, 84, 85
11:22	85
11:25	84, 85
11:28-9	84
11:29	66
11:32-33	85-86
11:33	180
12:2	51, 90, 104
12:2-3	166
12:4	131
12:9	29
13:4	179
13:8	32, 117
13:9	66
13:10	32
13:11-14	174
13:13	165
13:14	126
14:1-3	156
14:4	109, 145
14:4, 5	30, 56
14:10	56, 179
14:14	145
14:15	32
14:17	38, 132, 145
14:22, 23	56, 104-105, 113, 115
15:3	66
15:8	111
15:8-9	46
15:18	116
15:26	187
15:44	21
16:2	145
16:3	189
16:6	190
16:7	190
16:9	189
16:11	144
16:12-13	144-145, 190
16:22	6
16:26	112, 116

To the Corinthians I

1:1	189
1:6-9	77
1:7	174
1:8	143
1:11	190
1:13	188
1:18	22
1:18-2:16	161
1:24	57, 162
1:25	162
1:29	162
1:30	162, 194
2:4-5	23
2:6	162
2:7	163
2:8	66, 93, 137
2:12	29
2:13-14	163
2:15	36
3:1	108
3:1-3	161
3:3	164
3:14	115
3:21	162
4:5	60

Reference	Page
4:7-8	162
4:8	108
4:20	22
5:1-2	108
5:2-5	109
5:5	143
5:7	125
5:9	7
6:4	143
6:12	50, 108, 132
6:13	139
6:14	142
6:15-16	108, 139
6:19	140
6:20	131
7:1	60
7:3-4	190
7:17	90, 145
7:19	47, 90
7:20	142
7:22	145
7:23	147
7:28	123
7:29, 31	173, 174, 181
7:29-31	166
7:37	61
8:1-3	29
8:5	134, 143
8:7, 12	156
8:8	133
8:10	108, 133, 156
9:1	185, 193
9:1-18	195
9:2	144
9:5	55
9:13	112
9:14	66
9:19-23	133
10:1-11	134
10:8	134
10:9	142
10:11	174
10:12	108, 134
10:14	134
10:15	50
10:19-20	134
10:20	139
10:21	108, 134
10:22	142
10:23	29, 107
10:25	132, 143
10:27	132
10:29	155, 156
11:1	135, 195
11:2-16	135, 191
11:11-12	191
11:16	191
11:17	135
11:19-20	137
11:20	135
11:22	55
11:23-26	65, 135
11:25	136
11:26-27	137
11:29	137
11:31-32	109
12:3	37
12:8-11	38
12:13	131
12:15-18	131

12:27-28 138
13:7 .... 30, 55
13:8 .... 33, 160
13:9-10 160
13:11 .... 160, 165
13:12 33
13:13 25
13:23 55
13:33 191
13:13b-36 191
14:1 .... 30, 116, 169
14:12 .... 57, 14, 188
14:14-16 57
14:20 .... 50, 164, 175
14:25 60
14:28-33 133
14:29 52
14:36 55
14:40 57
15:3 27
15:3-7 66
15:12-19 175
15:20 175
15:21 144
15:23 176
15:24 174
15:24-28 174
15:27 54
15:28 142
15:29-34 176
15:31 177
15:32 178
15:34 50
15:35 55
15:35-50 177
15:39 120
15:42-44 121
15:44 40
15:45 .... 39, 121
15:49 182
15:51-55 177
15:56 90
16:12 189
16:14 30
16:19 189
16:21 6

To the Corinthians II
1:1 189
1:8-10 176
1:9-10 178
1:12 124
1:17 123
1:18 77
1:18-21 47
1:19 189
1:22 .... 40, 60
2:1 10
2:11 143
2:12 .... 19, 144
2:13 189
2:17 .... 55, 182
3 – 4 .... 19ff.
3:1 19
3:1-2 185
3:3 .... 87, 185
3:4-18 54
3:8 .... 36, 153
3:15 82
3:16 142

3:17	37, 146, 154
3:18	39, 178
3:21	50
4:3	19
4:4	143
4:4-6	182
4:5	144
4:6	35
4:7	24
4:10-11	177
4:11	194
4:14	142
4:16	166
4:17	40
4:18	182
5:3	130
5:4	130, 182
5:5	38, 40
5:7	165, 183
5:10	130, 179
5:11	142
5:14	142
5:14	33, 117, 167
5:16	65
5:17, 19	33, 124, 153
5:20	174
5:21	40
7:1	122
7:2	19
7:4	159
7:5-6	122
8 – 9	187
8:6, 23	189
8:9	143
8:12	50
8:16	189
9:8	115
10:1, 10	192
10:3	123, 165
10:5	142
10:7-8	192
10:8	144, 185
10:12	192
11:4-7	19
11:7-8	192
11:9, 11, 16	192
11:12-15	189
11:14, 15	143
11:23-28	10
12:2	130, 181
12:7	122
12:9	194
12:10	195
12:11	192
12:12	185
12:16	192
12:18	189
13:4	66, 194, 195
13:5-6	50
13:10	144

To the Galatians

1:1	193
1:4	40
1:6	105
1:6, 9, 11	19
1:7	106, 122, 148
1:10	19, 142, 193
1:12	185, 193
1:13	65

1:18	193
2:1	193
2:2	186
2:4	149
2:5	105, 149, 186
2:6, 9	186
2:8-10	187
2:11-14	186
2:12	106
2:14	148
2:15	101
2:19	94
2:20	66, 67, 125, 144
2:21	97, 148, 153
3:1	50, 107
3:2	36, 55, 97
3:2-3	148
3:3-9	106
3:14	5
3:15	54, 95
3:15-18	106
3:16	54
3:17	149
3:19	68, 94, 96, 117
3:21	90
3:22	89
3:23	94, 145
3:24-4:7	95
3:25	141
3:28	187
4:1	145
4:2	141
4:3	5, 94
4:3, 9	93
4:4	64, 111
4:5	149
4:6	60, 142
4:7	38, 149
4:8	93, 94, 145, 148, 159
4:13-5	122
4:14	195
4:15	55, 106
4:16	148
4:21	106
4:21-23	54, 150
4:24-29	150-151
5:1	153
5:4	97, 106
5:6	28, 47, 115
5:7	148
5:11-12	151-152, 193
5:13	126, 155
5:17	125
5:18	37, 97
5:19	160
5:19-24	106
5:22	28, 116, 126
5:23	93
5:24, 25	116, 125-126
5:26	107
6:1-2	107
6:4	115
6:8	127
6:11	122
6:11-18	6
6:15	47, 153
6:17	9, 122, 147

To the Philippians

1:1	189

1:9-10 53
1:10 ....174, 183
1:20 ....72, 130
1:23 130
1:27 ....23, 28, 39, 165, 181
2:2-5 53
2:6-7 144
2:6-11 ....68, 143, 195
2:7 63
2:8 66
2:12-13 168
2:15 168
2:20-22 189
3:1 145
3:3 40
3:6 72
3:8-9 ....67, 72, 142
3:10-12 72
3:11 168
3:13-16 169
3:17-19 170
3:20 ....142, 170, 174, 181
3:21 ....142, 178
4:1-2, 4 145
4:5 174
4:18 104

To the Thessalonians I
1:1 189
1:3 ....31, 145
1:4 29
1:5 ....19, 23, 56
1:8 67
1:10 179
2:3-6 193

2:4 60
2:7 160
2:11 160
2:14 66
2:19 ....143, 194
3:8 145
3:12 170
3:12-13 61
4:2-7 194
4:8 ....36, 54
4:14-17 180
4:15 174
4:17 173
5:19 ....31, 179
5:12 144
5:21-22 52
5:23 ....25, 38
5:24 77

To Philemon
passim 52
23 189

Also by Herold Weiss
from Energion Publications

For those who believe that one can be both scholarly and faithful, this is a 'must read' book!
Dr. Robert R. LaRochelle
UCC Pastor and author of
Crossing the Street

When Weiss walks you through the Gospel of John, the maze turns to amazement.
Abraham Terian
St. Nersess Armenian Seminary

More from Energion Publications

Personal Study

Finding My Way in Christianity	Herold Weiss	$16.99
Holy Smoke! Unholy Fire	Bob McKibben	$14.99
The Jesus Paradigm	David Alan Black	$17.99
When People Speak for God	Henry Neufeld	$17.99
The Sacred Journey	Chris Surber	$11.99

Christian Living

Faith in the Public Square	Robert D. Cornwall	$16.99
Grief: Finding the Candle of Light	Jody Neufeld	$9.99
Crossing the Street	Robert LaRochelle	$16.99
Life as Pilgrimage	David Moffett-Moore	14.99

Bible Study

From Inspiration to Understanding	Edward W. H. Vick	$24.99
Philippians: A Participatory Study Guide	Bruce Epperly	$12.99
Ephesians: A Participatory Study Guide	Robert D. Cornwall	$12.99

Theology

Creation in Scripture	Herold Weiss	$12.99
Creation: the Christian Doctrine	Edward W. H. Vick	$12.99
The Politics of Witness	Allan R. Bevere	$9.99
Ultimate Allegiance	Robert D. Cornwall	$9.99
History and Christian Faith	Edward W. H. Vick	$9.99
The Journey to the Undiscovered Country	William Powell Tuck	$9.99
Philosophy for Believers	Edward W. H. Vick	14.99
Process Theology	Bruce G. Epperly	$5.99

Ministry

Clergy Table Talk	Kent Ira Groff	$12.99
Thrive	Ruth Fletcher	$14.99

Generous Quantity Discounts Available
Dealer Inquiries Welcome
Energion Publications — P.O. Box 841
Gonzalez, FL 32560
Website: http://energion.com
Phone: (850) 525-3916

www.ingramcontent.com/pod-product-compliance
Lightning Source LLC
LaVergne TN
LVHW041541070426
835507LV00011B/858